The Witch

A Book of S[illegible]dows;
Earthguard Wicca

Eileen Smith/Lady Cara

CAPALL BANN PUBLISHING

www.capallbann.co.uk

The Witches' Heart

Book 1

Wiccan Manual for Solitary and Group Practitioners

ISBN 186163 261 4

Cover design by Paul Mason

Published by:

Capall Bann Publishing
Auton Farm
Milverton
Somerset
TA4 1NE

This book is dedicated to my Mom, my children Maryanne and Dennis, my Dad who gave me the courage to be myself, to my Grandchildren: Matthew, Sean, Jason, Justin, Peter, Amber, and my great granddaughters Aaliyah and Kayleigh Morgan both born 2005.

To my teacher Lady Elsbeth,
Patricia Crowther, a teacher and dear friend.
To my best friend and first High Priest, Michael Thorn

I also dedicate it to my High Priest Bacchus, Lady Diana my Maiden and Deputy, and my Coven, Path of the Pentacle, Path of the Sacred Grove, Path of the Sacred Pentagram and Grail Keepers Grove for all their help.

To my friend who once said to me:
"When are you going to write your book?"
Dwina Murphy Gibb.

And to R.J. Stewart another teacher and inspiration
Who told me I could do this.

Thank You All.

Contents

The Introduction	1
Chapter 1 The Call of the Ancient Ones	27
Chapter 2 Your First Steps On the Path	33
Chapter 3 Circles Basics	55
Chapter 4 Your First Steps with Ritual	71
Chapter 5 Working with Ritual	90
Chapter 6 Seasonal Rituals	103
Chapter 7 Additional Rituals	146
Chapter 8 Magickal Workings	166
Chapter 9 Meditations	197
The Best Wiccan Suppliers I know	207
In Conclusion	208

Lady Cara 1971

The Introduction
Journey with the Author

How to use this Book of Shadows

EarthGuard Wicca is a tradition that began in 1998. It has traditional energies similar to Gardnerian, but it is more for the masses than for the priesthood. Its groups can vary in size from three to twenty-three. Its teachings are more earth combination moon oriented. We worship the gods and goddesses of the universe. Goddess Gaia - the earth, Goddess Diana - the moon, Herne - the father god of humans and animals.

The focus is on working with nature, its cycles and energies combined with your own. As you begin to tune into nature you will find yourself tuning into yourself as well. The growth cycles the earth goes through, people also experience. We don't normally notice this growth from day to day. Wicca helps us tune into this growth pattern. It also teaches us how to make adjustments when we feel out of balance. One of the keys is within the pentagram. As we work with this symbol it teaches us about the importance of balance within our lives. The pentagram is a symbol of balance and protection. We view it not only as a shield of protection but the containment of the four elements, including spirit in perfect balance within a circle that has no beginning or ending. At the top of the four elements is the spirit of man or woman in complete balance maintaining that elemental balance. To experience balance in one's life is to experience power. To strive to understand oneself is to connect with the pentagram. Later in this book is a section where you will begin to work on this understanding. It is called "Discovering Self Through the Elements, The

Discovery Book." This is considered part of level one in EarthGuard.

This tradition has five levels of learning with a dedication, initiation and three elevations.

The Five Levels of Knowledge in EarthGuard Wicca

Level One: Dedication to the gods, goddesses and nature.

Discovery of self through the elements.
Creating and working with rituals.
The gathering of your personal tools.

Level Two: Initiation through the inner earth.

Working with your inner guides and the faery world.
Journey with the Goddess Gaia.
Connecting with the earth's core in conjunction with your own core.
Learning self healing.

Level Three: Elevation into the earth's vegetation and tree energies.

Experiencing the worlds of wood faeries, gnomes and dryads.
Finding and journeying with your faery guides.
Journeying with the Horned God Herne.

Level Four: Elevation into the oceans, rivers, streams and lakes.

Working with the undines.
Journeying with Moon Goddess Diana.
Working with your own ancestral system.
Learning how to heal others.
This is the level of elder.

Level Five: Elevation into the microcosm.

Experiencing the planetary forces.
Working with the ancient teachers of the craft.
This is the level of teacher.

The first book will acquaint you with the rituals of EarthGuard Wicca, along with the first level of dedication. The second book will take you through levels two through five, bringing you through the tradition. This is a true journey with self, nature and the gods.

I've been a teacher of witchcraft since 1975 in the Gardnerian Tradition. I found this path in the early'70s after moving back to Long Island, N.Y. from Florida. I had just been divorced and was starting a new life. I had no idea that would include my spiritual side as well. On a Sunday afternoon driving through Bayshore, a small sign on a third floor of a building caught my eye. It said "Witchcraft Museum." I did a u-turn and drove down a side street to find an old two-story house that was converted into a museum. This house brought to mind movies I had seen. I just knew I had to see what was inside. Unfortunately, it was closed, but it had a mailbox I could leave a message in. I left a note saying I was interested in seeing the museum and would like to know when it would be open. I included my phone number in the hope of a call.

A week went by, but no phone call came. I visited several times after that hoping to catch it open, but never did. After leaving about five messages I decided it was not meant to be. So I put it aside and forgot about it. One afternoon the phone rang and my sister Cathy answered it. My children and I were living with her and her family for a while until I was ready to get my own place again. She turned to me with a surprised look and said a man with a British accent was on the phone asking for me. I couldn't imagine who it was since I had just moved back to New York and hadn't made any new friends. When I answered the phone I heard a soft-spoken British voice say to me, "I'm Raymond Buckland. I own the Witchcraft Museum, and it will be opened Saturday if you are interested in seeing it." To say the least I was very surprised to receive the call. Enough time had passed that I figured the museum was closed for good. I thanked him for calling me and told him

I would be there Saturday. Most students of the craft today know this man's writings. Back then his book wasn't in the neighborhood bookstores. It was at his museum that I first saw it.

The following week seemed to crawl by. When Saturday came I made sure I would be there as soon as the museum opened. When I walked in, Raymond Buckland was standing behind the counter. He was an interesting looking man, small in stature with a goatee. I told him I was the woman he phoned the other day. He said, "Oh, you're the lady who left all the notes." Another woman came in, so we didn't speak until after I went through the museum.

It cost $1 to walk through. I paid my fee, and he showed me the way. I took the stairs to the second floor. There was a mannequin dressed like a magician standing in the center of a circle. On the wall was a large black mirror. I had such a strong feeling about peering into it, but it was roped off and I was afraid I would get caught. Downstairs were witches' tools in a glass case. There were many other things, but I don't remember what they were.

There was a book that caught my attention. It was black, and was entitled "Book of Shadows." I couldn't imagine what was inside it, so I asked Mr. Buckland if I could see it. He said without hesitation, "No," explaining that was only for initiates. Being a Scorpio, I had to ask why. This led into a conversation about the religion of the craft. The other woman had left, so he had time to talk to me. This was the first time I heard someone speak of witchcraft in this way. I was intrigued by what he had to say. At the time I met him I was on a long journey in search of the right religion for me. Nothing I tried seemed to work. I was brought up a Roman Catholic, which never felt right. The only things I liked about it were the ritual at a high mass, incense and candles. That wasn't enough to keep me there. I began a spiritual quest by experiencing different sects of Christianity and Judaism. They all seemed the same in different ways.

From there I looked into the Eastern philosophies. Being brought up in an Irish household, it seemed too foreign. My personal philosophy was, it needs to feel as if I just came home. Nothing made me feel that way. Now here I was in a museum of witchcraft speaking to a witch about his religion. I wondered, how in God's name did I get here? I've since learned the Goddess works in strange ways.

After many questions, Raymond Buckland gave me a post office box to write to. It was to a Lady Theos, a high priestess who lived on Long Island. He said if I was serious about the craft this priestess would be able to help me. I bought his book "Witchcraft from the Inside," and it was there my journey began. I wrote to Lady Theos for about two months hoping for a connection. It wasn't easy back then. Most people who were involved in the craft were underground. Others who were involved brought in most people who were in groups. I was someone who didn't know anyone, so it was a waiting game.

Just when I thought it was hopeless I received a call from another high priestess who lived in Bayshore. Her name was Lady Elsbeth. She was starting a new group and had received my name from Lady Theos. It took a while before I met with her and her high priest, who was her husband. They required a certain amount of books to be read to ensure that I knew what I was getting involved in. They suggested Mr. Buckland's book and books on mythology and ancient customs. There wasn't much you could find in the early '70s. Today there are so many books you can read on the subject as well as people you can meet. And there is the Internet, which is a harvest of knowledge on the craft. I consumed the books that were available like they were chocolate. Many phone calls and conversations followed. I could feel that this was possibly the path I was seeking.

Meeting Elsbeth was an exciting moment for me. I didn't know what to expect. Driving there was a journey in itself. I was given easy directions, but as I drew near I couldn't find the house. I spent more than an hour searching and going in circles before I found it. I must have passed the house ten times before the address was in clear sight. It was as though it was invisible to me for a time, and if I was to find it I had to persevere or it would be lost to me. I had to keep searching until I found it, and finally there it was as she said in plain sight. The house was a large two-story with high dense hedges all around. As I walked toward the hedges it felt as if I were stepping into another realm. When I knocked on the door I was very nervous. It must have been reflected in my expression because later she asked me if I expected her to answer the door on a broom?

Elsbeth is a small woman with beautiful long dark chestnut-colored hair to her waist. She had one baby on her hip and two other small children playing in the living room. Her husband was sitting at a dinning room table that was filled with paper work. He was an engineer on the Long Island Railroad. They invited me in and offered me a cup of coffee. As I looked around I thought to myself, "In passing I would never believe they were witches." Her high priest Exolar interviewed me. After much conversation and a pot or two of coffee they felt comfortable enough in inviting me to their upcoming circle. It was going to be a sabbat. There would be many people there and all were expected to bring a covered dish of food for the feast that followed. I asked what it would cost to attend. I was on a limited budget. She said nothing but the food to share and something to drink. He turned to me and said, "Money never crossed the palms in witchcraft, and it was a shared religion." Because of my finances at that time this was a relief. I would be happy to cook something to share. Circle would be the following week, so I had time to prepare.

I will never forget my first circle. I was told that they worshipped skyclad. I didn't understand at first, but in the next sentence they told me that meant worshipping in the nude. You were clad with the sky. I know it was the '70s, but I was a one-time Catholic girl who was very shy about her body. Not to mention being overweight. When I was married I never even undressed in front of my husband. At night if I had to use the bathroom, I would wrap a sheet or blanket around myself. God forbid my husband would see me naked without having sex. So the idea of being naked with a lot of people I had never met was not pleasant. I thought to myself; how am I going to do this? Was it worth it?

Well, here I was on the night of my first circle. It was at Lady Elsbeth's house. I arrived early. Only one other person was there before me, and she was a size 6. But I was relieved to see someone else there. I was happy to have someone to talk to. Her name was Tansy. This was the name she chose for herself. In the craft it is customary to choose a magickal name. She was a single mother like myself, so we had things in common. My high priestess didn't have time to make conversation with us since she was busy getting ready for the celebration. Tansy became interested in the craft after meeting a practitioner. It made sense to her. This was one of the reasons I was attracted to it myself.

The front door opened and people started flowing in. I thought to myself, if only one person who walked through that door was overweight I would be eternally grateful. It didn't happen, but the Goddess sent one person who would put my fears to rest. A woman in her late sixties came in who was about 5 feet 6 and about 98 pounds. I thought if she had the courage to experience this, so could I.

I noticed that no one knocked before they came in. When I asked about that, I was told on a circle night the door is left open for people to come in because all were family. Also it was less noticeable to neighbors if everyone just quietly enters without knocking.

There were about 25 people who came that evening. I was amazed that so many people were interested in witchcraft as a religion. There were people from different covens. Some traveled long distances to attend the sabbat. I felt a little lost not knowing them. They were greeting each other with hugs and the witchcraft greeting "blessed be." Many hadn't seen each other for some time, and you could see the joy in their faces as they embraced.

I was introduced to everyone, and all gave me a hug and said, "blessed be." I never experienced that many hugs at one time in my life. I felt very welcome. When it was time for circle everyone went upstairs. The circle was held in a bedroom that was converted into a temple room. Everyone was getting ready in the room across the hall from the temple. I was apprehensive about joining them. Getting ready meant taking off my clothes. It was my first big test. I hid behind the door and did a Gypsy Rose Lee, slowly disrobing. I noticed people talking and no one was noticing or thinking anything about it. It occurred to me that I was the only one worried. No one was eyeing anyone, and it all felt quite natural. So I joined the group as they waited to enter the temple room. It was quite amazing to me: Here I was standing with a group of people without a stitch of clothing on, and I felt perfectly natural. If anyone had told me I was going to do this I would have said they were out of their minds. Yet here I was.

I think every movie I ever saw about witches and witchcraft came flowing into my mind. I thought, I still have time to leave if I wanted to. What a great time to think of this after I had taken off my clothes. But I thought if I leave now I would never know what this was about. Since I was able to go this far I might as well go the rest of the way. Here was my second test, and you know tests usually come in threes.

I walked through the door and could see a black trunk sitting in the center of a circle that was marked with four candles, one at each of the four directions. The trunk had a beautiful white cloth, a sword, salt, water and two lighted candles on it. This was the altar for the circle. At first the altar seemed too low, but I soon realized it was the right height so everyone could see each other when seated. There was a point in the ceremony when everyone sat and shared wine and cookies. Lady Elsbeth took this time to explain everything that transpired and we were free to ask questions. It was the social time of the circle. The thing I noticed was that once Lady Elsbeth cast the circle that feeling I had been seeking came to me. I felt as if I had just come home. The third test for me was that realization. To this day it remains that way in my heart. I became a member of the outer court group for the Bayshore Coven that night and I never realized it would change my life in so many ways.

Once I made the commitment to join it was time for me to choose a craft name. That was interesting, choosing a name I wanted. When I was a child I never liked my name and used to pretend that I had other names. I eventually learned to love my name Eileen because it was my Nana's name and she was a very special lady in my life.

I was told I needed a magickal name to mark my new life in the craft. After a lot of thought and reading I chose the name of Cara. Its meaning is friend and dear one. Friendship has always been very important to me. I worked in what was called an outer court group for just under a year. The outer court group is where you learn many things but mostly whether or not this is your path. After the first circle I had no doubts. I felt as if I had done this before, not in this life but definitely in another. Once I became a member of the group I was able to meet so many others who saw things the way I did and experienced life the way I do.

I remember one Samhain gathering around 1975 with about 200 witches from all over the country. It was a very special night. Not only was it a grand All Hallows party, but Lady Rowen (Raymond Buckland's ex-wife) handed her coven and sword over to Lady Theos. It was an amazing experience because it is rare to witness such an event. Lady Theos didn't know it was going to happen, which made it more exciting. Most everyone present was from the same family line in our tradition. Being part of the Gardnerian tradition has been an ongoing education. I consider myself very lucky to have met the right people my first time out.

My high priestess' Queen and Magus, Lady Theos and Phoenix, initiated me into the Gardnerian tradition in October 1973. Lady Elsbeth and Exolar were not third degree at that time, so they were not yet able to initiate anyone. My coven leaders adhered strictly to their traditions, which is the glue that keeps things together. I respect that aspect of the Gardnerian tradition. I would have preferred that they initiate me, but it was a great honor to be initiated by her high priest and priestess.

My journey with Elsbeth, Exolar and my coven was amazing. The group truly was a family. Over time we became very much in tune with each other. Spiritual connections between people can be some of the strongest bonds you can have. When someone had a problem the rest of the group could feel it. I can remember having a really bad day. My phone rang and it was a member of my group: "Ok, what's happening? You came into my mind so strong I had to call. What's going on?" It always amazed me when this happened. It never failed. You always have the feeling you're never alone. In most cases you don't have to ask. They come to you with help or support.

The healing bonds are even stronger. I had a growth in my thigh. It was very painful. I went to the hospital to get it checked. The doctor told me it was a cyst. Because it was too deep to come to the surface, he would have to cut it out. They didn't know if it was a staph infection, so they put me in my own section with a private nurse. Istar, a member of my Coven came to see me. She told me the group was meeting that night to do a healing. I was part of many healings over the years, but never before a recipient. That night a miracle happened. It was about 10:30 when all the lights in my unit went out along with my TV. It didn't happen anywhere else in the hospital except in my unit. At the same time the pain stopped. I rang for the nurse. She came in to look at it and told me the cyst had come to the surface and released. She couldn't believe it, but there it was. My doctor had a late surgery and stopped in to take a look at me after she left him a message. He shrugged his shoulders and didn't know what to say because he thought it was impossible for it to come to the surface on its own. He still felt it would be better to operate to ensure everything was out so it would not return. I knew that night that all would be well. One of the main teachings in the craft is about healing oneself and others. I was lucky to experience that first hand.

After two more years of training, in 1975 fellow coven member Michael Thorn and I started our own coven, named Path of the Pentacle. We worked very hard and very well together. Michael is a very intelligent, well-read and dedicated man. He was interested in the craft from the age of sixteen. I remember my high priest talking about him at circle. He was guiding him until Michael turned eighteen and could enter the coven. We hit it off as soon as we met. We were both attending the same university. Michael was studying to be a nurse and I was in the field of entomology. Michael went on to earn a degree in psychology and a master's in business. He is special in many ways. I remember the evening he decided to come out of the closet. After circle one evening, having coffee and doughnuts at my priestess' dining room table, Michael made a grand announcement in the middle of a conversation. "I'm gay," he said. The only reaction he received was, "And?"

In other religions homosexuality was frowned upon. In the craft, the Goddess says in her charge, "All acts of love are my rituals." You are born whom you are, and the gods do not make mistakes. In ancient times people who were gay where considered highly spiritual. Makes you wonder about the direction spirituality has taken.

As our friendship grew we decided that we were a good combination to work as magickal partners. Michael is a Pisces and I am a Scorpio, two water signs. We had an equal drive for knowledge. When it is time to start a coven, people just seem to find you. It is as though the Goddess whispers in their ear and points the way. When you connect with the right people you can feel that family connection as though you were together once before in another time and place. It all seems so familiar. This is a gift the Goddess gives us, to be able to worship as a family, and after we die to be reborn and meet again and love again in that family. You know and feel it in your heart when you are once more with your magickal family.

Working with Michael was a magickal experience that formed a connection for life to death and life again. I am sure of this. After I moved back to Florida, Michael started his own coven that became very fruitful. Path of the Pentacle moved with me in 1978 to Hollywood, Fla. This was the first Gardnerian coven to be established in Florida. I placed an ad in Circle Network News, a pagan/wiccan newspaper that went all over the country. As in New York, when I was ready to open the coven to new members, people came from all over the state. Path of the Pentacle has initiated 54 members to date. Out of these initiates fifteen new covens were born and continue to grow. Our family is large and as close as any blood family could be. We continue to meet for major sabbats and family celebrations.

Then in the mid 1980s I was given the address of Patricia Crowther. She is one of the best-known witches in England. Gerald Gardner, the man who brought witchcraft out in the open initiated her. Like Gerald Gardner, she authored many books on the craft, including *Lid Off the Cauldron*, *Witch Blood*, *Zodiac Experience*, *One Witches World*, *High Priestess*, *Life and Times of Patricia Crowther*, and *Witches Were for Hanging*. After corresponding with her for a few years, I traveled to England with a couple of my coven members to meet her.

It was incredible to experience sacred sites such as Stonehenge and Glastonbury after reading about them. But the highlight of the trip was meeting Patricia. She lives in Sheffield in northern England. It's an industrial city, but it has some of the most beautiful parks and countryside you could imagine, and their antique shops are outstanding.

Patricia is an elegant, statuesque woman with a great presence. Our first meeting we spent a wonderful afternoon in her home talking about the Craft. In her sitting room were numerous photographs of herself and Gerald Gardner. Everywhere you looked you could see statues of the Goddess in all her forms. It was obvious that Patricia was dedicated to the work of the Goddess.

Many visits followed over the years, and working with her has been an incredible experience. Getting to know Patricia and Ian, her consort and life-mate, is one of my most valued treasures. Patricia and Ian have taken me to visit sacred sites most people didn't know existed. There was one I will keep in my heart always. I still go there sometimes in my meditations. It is an ancient stone circle with burial mounds that you could feel before you even approached. It took my breath away when I first set eyes on it. I understand some people still worship there at festival times.

Patricia and Ian walking the circle at Arbor Low

We first drove a long distance out into the countryside, then stopped for lunch at a wonderful little cottage that was converted into a restaurant. It was white with a thatched roof and dark wooden shutters. If I were to create a witch's cottage it would look like that. After lunch we drove further into farm and cattle country. Across from a field of cows was a sign that marked the entrance to the stone circles site, Arbor Low. If you didn't know it was there you would never find it. There were stone walls that separated the fields. We had to climb over a couple walls that were about three feet high. It had a few steps, so it wasn't too difficult. Next we had to climb up a steep hill and walk through a herd of cows before we came to the stone circle. Since I walk with a cane, this was quite a journey for me.

There were two large stones to mark the entrance into the circle. Then there were stones from ancient times that formed the circle, which was surrounded by a moat. In the center of the circle was a large stone altar. You could sit there if you desired. I so desired. I closed my eyes and hoped for a vision. What I saw I will keep to myself. We walked the circle, and images formed in my mind of rituals and people in costumes. It was impressive.

Each year I visited Patricia we went to a different sacred site. It was enchanting to listen to her speak of these places. Her knowledge of them and the events of the past were interesting and enlightening. You could almost feel yourself in the history of the land.

In 1991, Patricia and Ian agreed to visit me in Florida. She lectured on witchcraft in my store, Magical Forest. People flew in from all parts of the country to meet and speak with her. My store was about 1,200 square feet, and there wasn't even standing room left by the time the workshop began. Many of the craft people wished to spend time with Patricia and Ian while they were here. They stayed a fortnight, as Patricia would say. They loved Florida. It was the end of October and the Goddess blessed us with fine weather.

Before they left I arranged for them to meet with Dwina Murphy Gibb. I met Dwina in the early 80's at a Samhain gathering. She is a very spiritual woman with an Irish heart who's smile and kindness could warm the world. Dwina is the first woman in 300 years that was crowned patroness of the Druids in England. If you meet Dwina, you will not soon forget her. She is a well-known artist, author and is married to a famous rock star, Robin Gibb of the Bee Gees. It was such a treat when she accepted my invitation to our Samhain Festival.

From left to right: Patricia Crowther and myself at one of England's enchanted forests.

Most of the people who came to Patricia's lecture came to the festival. There were about 125 attendees. One of the rituals and magick reflected the cruelty humans put upon animals. The magick was directed at a farm in England that was importing monkeys for the purpose of experiments. Patricia had an on going project with other craft people in England to close down the farm. Patricia is famous for her work with animal rights. In the ritual Patricia played the Goddess and several craft people took the roles of different animal species on the earth. They pleaded their cases of mans cruelty and asked for her aid. She blessed them and led an energy raising that transcended time and space. I stood in the center with Patricia back to back with our swords directing the energy raised. As long as I live I will never forget that magickal working. I get chills whenever I think about it. Two weeks after she returned home she sent me a newspaper clipping that showed the closing down of the business and the monkeys being sent to a safe haven. Its great to get a confirmation about your magickal work, but to see it in print was amazing.

Dwina led us in an ancient Druid chant that evening that raised the hair on the back of my neck. It was as if you were being lifted up in the tones. As she began all who were there chimed in. Over 100 people chanting together focused on the Lord of the underworld.

A few days after the festival Donna, Dwina's secretary arranged for all of us to meet at Dwina's home in Miami Beach. Dwina thought it was important for us to meet with a Miccosukee Indian spiritual leader. She had connected with them after Hurricane Andrew. They were hit pretty badly, and no one was doing anything to help them. I had some local people call me about their problem. Dwina called and asked me if I knew anyone who needed help. Her and her husband Robbin were ready and willing to help anyone who was in need. So the connection was made, and they bought

From left to right, Patricia Crowther and Dwina Murphy Gibb at the 1991 Samhain Festival

truckloads of supplies down to the reservation. It was amazing to see such gener-osity. Dwina is a woman who lives her spirituality. Through this she got to know the spiritual leader of the tribe. She told me how similar our religions were.

We had lunch with them on the reservation and spoke openly about our religions without saying what they were. Their meaning for the word witch was very different from ours. It was amazing how close our belief systems were. It was like a meeting of the spirits. All barriers dropped and a connection of the mind and spirit took place. After the luncheon Dwina took us on a airboat ride with the Indians in the everglades. That was an experience for both Patricia and myself.

After a two-week visit with Patricia and Ian it was difficult to say goodbye. But wonderful bonds and friendships were formed that I'm sure will last a lifetime. My friendship with Patricia has grown over the years, and she still amazes me with her knowledge of the Goddess and the ancient ones.

In the mid-1990s, a promoter for R.J. Stewart contacted me to see if I was interested in having him at my store for workshops. I was a fan of his books and was excited to meet him. He's a Scottish author of more than 40 books and tapes on Traditional Celtic, classical mythological traditions and the faery and underworld traditions. His knowledge of England's history and myths is impressive, but his knowledge of the faery underworld is even more so. He has restored the working tradition of the faery world within the underworld for people to be able to work with their ancestral spiritual paths. At one of his workshops I recall a meditation that took us to the underworld, and at the same time brought us back so we were experiencing both at the same time. It was an experience I will never forget. R.J. Stewart is also a musician with a voice that can enchant you. At one of his concerts he sang an ancient magical ballad that gave the impression he had come from that place.

Bob and I began a friendship, and he became a regular at my store for a couple of years. We spent time talking about the craft and working with the faery world over many dinners. Bob also reads tarot cards, and I always arranged time for a reading. He had his own method and his own deck that he designed called the *Dream Power Tarot*. His readings were some of the most accurate I have ever had. In one of the readings he told me I was going to start a new business. I thought he was way off base. During that same visit to Florida he did a reading for Fran, my future partner, and told her similar things. She didn't believe him either because she didn't want a partner in her jewelry designing business. Soon after he left, Fran came into my store to sell me some of her

R. J. Stewart

pieces of jewelry. I had a design I wanted to produce, so I asked her if she could do it for me. She was happy to help. When she brought the finished piece back, I said to her, "Would you like to go into business together?" At first she said no because she thought I wanted her for the retail store. When she realized it was a new wholesale jewelry business I was talking about, we sat down and put it together. We've been in business with Blue Moon Spiritual Accessories for seven years, just as Bob predicted.

One year his family came to Florida with him, and I was able to show them Disney World in Orlando. We got to know each other very well during that visit. At another time we got together to bring a group of people to England for a spiritual experience. We all stayed at a wonderful metaphysical retreat in Somerset that is close to Glastonbury, the spiritual Mecca of England. During the day Bob would take us to various spiritual places. One morning we went to Avery, a town that was built within three stone circles. Bob took us to the main circle and walked us to each stone while playing his flute. We truly felt that we were with the Pied Piper. He then led us on meditations for each of the stones. He spoke of the history and myths of this very magickal place. You could almost feel yourself back in another time. Some days he held workshops taking us into other worlds of the faery realm. One meditation took us to the Glastonbury Thor. We experienced it first spiritually, and the following day he took us there physically. We all could feel the Thor before we climbed it. We also had a visit from Paddy Slade, a well-known witch who wrote the book *Seasonal Magic; Diary of a Village Witch*. She spoke about World War II and working her craft during that time. Her stories were fascinating. This trip will remain in my mind and heart as one of the most spiritual vacations I ever had.

The experiences I had at Bob's workshops were inspirational to me. There is more to learn in the magickal world than one can imagine. This is a realm that you can feel, not just believe in. Bob does workshops all over the United States. His books are widely read and are some of the most interesting in the magickal field. He once said to me, "If you want to write a book, then pick a time of day and every day spend at least one hour working on it. Even if you just reread it and edit, you must work on it at that time. It will then become a reality." His encouragement and wise words have helped me many a day. If you are interested in reading his books, you can find them on the Internet at RJStewart.net. In your studies with EarthGuard, I highly recommend you read his *Initiation into the Underworld*, *Earth Lights* and *Power Within the Land*. These wonderful books on the faery tradition and the underworld are a good basis in understanding inner earth spirituality.

In the early '70s I met Margot Adler at a Samhain gathering on Long Island. She sang and played her guitar. In later years we met at several pagan gatherings. Subsequently, I received a call from my friend in New York informing me that Margot would be interested in doing Goddess workshops at my store. I was happy to reconnect with her. At least seventeen years had passed since I last saw her. I had always admired her intellect and energy. Margot wrote one of the most widely read books on the craft called *Drawing Down the Moon*. In the first edition of the book are pictures of my High Priestess Lady Elsbeth and High Priest Exolar, as well as myself and other coven members. I was living in Florida when her book came out. I didn't know that my picture would be in it, and it was quite a surprise to see a picture of myself dancing naked with my coven in the woods. I had forgotten about those pictures, which were originally taken in New York for another book. Happily that particular picture wasn't included in the second edition, thank the Goddess. Owning a bookstore has been wonderful because of the incredible people I met along the way, and Margot was one of them.

I was initiated into the Georgian tradition of the craft in early 1983. I met a high priestess called Lady Thea and her husband, High Priest Faffner, through a wonderful man from the Florida Keys. When I first moved to Florida I worked as a solitary for about a year, and then longed for a craft connection. The craft is family, and to be by yourself is very lonely. The craft is something you share, and it's difficult to do it alone. There wasn't much activity in Florida at that time. There were a couple of metaphysical bookstores, but no craft groups to speak of. That's when I placed the ad in Circle Network News. In a short time I received a letter from a man in the Florida Keys. That was at least a four-hour drive from where I lived in Hollywood, Fla., but that didn't matter to Edwyon, who was used to traveling. He was just happy to meet another craft person in South Florida. Edwyon was a large man with black hair and clear blue eyes. He was a captain who guided the large cruise ships past the coral reefs in the keys. Ed always wore jeans with suspenders. He had a large stomach so they never quite fit him. Every time he bent over you could see the top of the crack of his behind. Ed loved to wear his Sloppy Joe's T-shirt. He gave the impression of being a homeless person, but he certainly wasn't that. Edwyon was - he passed on to the Summerland in September 2001 - a brilliant man who could quote book after book. Edwyon received his doctorate in business just before he died. To know Edwyon was to love him. He was very special and a very powerful witch. To say the least, he touched my heart.

Edwyon was working with Lady Thea and Faffner in Bradenton on the Gulf Coast of Florida when I met him. I had just begun a group with a few people who found me through the local bookstores. Lady Thea invited us for a Beltane celebration. She and her family lived on ten acres of prime land that had been in her family for a couple of generations. Her home was old Floridian, one floor, all made of wood. I can still hear that sound the wooden floor made when you walked across it. Behind her house was an artesian well. There were giant elephant leaf plants everywhere. Her circle was deep in the woods on her property, accessible by a winding road. Along the way were huge Florida oak trees with long hanging vines. It was so enchanting to walk through. You felt the presence of the gnomes and faeries there. At night there were candlelit lanterns that showed the way to the circle in an area surrounded by oak trees. It was enchanting. A stone statue of the Goddess and a stone statue of the god Pan marked the opening to the circle. Their altar was set north of the circle, and there was a large fire pit to the south. The candles and the roaring fire illuminated the area. What an incredible sight.

We soon realized that we had a lot in common craft-wise. The group was of the Georgian tradition. In the years to follow we would meet every Beltane and Samhain. We would travel to them on Beltane and they to us for Samhain. We began to recognize each other as family. Then came the day we would cross initiate each other for the purpose of sharing family unity. This family unity exists to this day. Two of their students, Lady Rowen and Orion, began a journey with us of the Gardnerian tradition that would become very fruitful for both traditions. They have hived a number of covens of both Georgian and Gardnerian for the Goddess' family. Lady Rowen and Orion are two dedicated leaders of the craft today.

In the mid '80s I was drawn to the Golden Dawn. It wasn't that I was unhappy with what I was doing, but I felt there was more to this universe to explore. For years I would find books on the subject of ceremonial magick It was always of interest to me, but I never met anyone who actually practiced it. I felt strongly that I needed a teacher if I was going to pursue this. One day an invitation came in the mail at my store and one to my Lady Cara post office box. This was a sign to me that it must be time. When the student is ready the teacher comes. It was an invitation from my teacher, David Cherubim. His order was associated with the Israel Regardie Foundation in Los Angeles. I worked with David via the mail and phone for some time. Then I was invited to come to Los Angeles to be initiated into the Thelemic Order of the Golden Dawn.

It was a very exciting time for me. David told me that Christopher Hyatt would be participating in my initiation. He is a very well known psychologist and author, and was the head of the order. I never thought I would be meeting him, let alone have him as one of the officers at my initiation. I flew to Los Angeles and received my Neophyte and Zelotor initiations. The experience was extremely powerful, enlightening and spiritual. It was held at an antique furniture store. Some of the antiques were from the 16th Century, and many were far older then that. The rear of the store had been arranged to look as if you were back in medieval times. When I arrived I was told I would be initiated with another student. A large number of people were arriving who were members of the order. I had no idea what was going to happen, and I hoped I would be ready for this. I will never forget that day even if I live to be 150. I didn't need a plane to get home or even a broom for that matter; I could have flown on my own. That's how I felt. Although it wasn't witchcraft, it was a very magickal and spiritual experience. I'm still a member of the order in good standing.

Over the years I have interacted with priests and priestesses of many different traditions. Being a Scorpio with a Libra rising and a Leo moon, it has been a wonderfully intense path of learning. I've had many people cross my path who were looking for serious teachings but didn't want the priesthood. They also had a problem with skyclad, so I created EarthGuard Wicca. We wear street clothes when worshipping outdoors and robes when in our homes. There is a freedom that comes with wearing street clothes in parks. No one looks at you as if you are doing something strange. No one complains about your activities. It seems to work well for us. EarthGuard also can be taught and shared with your children, families and friends. With the priesthood and witchcraft, that isn't possible.

This book will give you a good basis to understand and practice Wicca. It will take you step by step through what you need to know in order to start or add to what you already have. It will tell you how to put it all together. There are clear and concise steps on choosing your name, preparing yourself for ritual and creating a sacred space. There is a section on tools you will need and how to consecrate them. You will learn how to erect your temple and prepare your altar. An important step is your dedication into the craft. It is the first step through the door of knowledge. Once you take it you will find yourself opening up to the teachings. This manual starts with the first things you need and continues with each step, so there isn't any guesswork. It is easy to follow.

There are meditations, sabbats, full moon and dark moon rituals and chants. There is a reference index in the back where you can learn about getting supplies. Book Two will cover extensive work with nature and the four other levels of knowledge. It will take you step by step through working on yourself through nature. Look for it in the future. If you are looking for an EarthGuard group to work with or just looking for someone to practice with, feel free to write me and I will be happy to refer you to people in your area. If you have any questions this book couldn't answer, feel free to contact me at:

Eileen Smith
Enchanted Forest Books and Gifts
11326 Semivole Blvd
Largo, Florida 33778
USA

Good luck on your journey, and may the Goddess forever guide your path.

Blessed be, Lady Cara

Chapter 1

The Call of the Ancient Ones

Seekers

The seeker's path is unmarked, un-trodden and long forgotten. So the prophecy continues unspoken but never lost. The way of the Goddess has been since the beginning of time and is in the hearts of all special people. Only the strong and open may step upon her path.

Do you hear the calls of your ancestors to become aware of all that is around you? Then take the step.

On earth those of the Wiccan path walk this journey. They see themselves as a part of this land and of the universe as a whole. Their journey is that of a guide for themselves and the generations that follow. The earth is beautiful and simple when left alone to its own making. People make the journey complicated. Nature isn't complicated. It is simple and pure. All must be experienced with the senses and felt with the heart. All life must be respected and revered. All animals are our kindred spirits. We must strive to understand them and feel the connection we have with them. Most people are disconnected from nature. Most people place themselves above nature, the earth and animals. At one time they had the connection but lost it due to arrogance. It is time for the children of the Goddess to come home and be a part of all that is. Balance and harmony are the keys to all things.

The Wiccan knows to disturb as little as possible in nature. They take the time to journey with as much of nature as possible. Those of the craft will share with all who would listen but never push it on anyone who is not open to the journey. You must seek them out. Only those who have the ears to hear will understand the message. You are but a voice of the distant lands in time and space. The journey is yours as soon as you take your first step. The question is whether you have the vision or not. Can you feel that tap on your shoulder that is calling for your attention; there must be more to life then what I can see.

Wicca the Path of Nature and the Ancient Ones

Wicca brings with it a responsibility to oneself and nature. It is a path of discovery through nature. Be aware that your life will change once you step upon this path. There is nothing on earth like it.

Some call it a nature religion, but it is a way of life, a way of looking at life, and a way of experiencing life. You must live within the laws of nature. So you must be a keen observer of nature.

There is a three-fold law of retribution that states, "What ever you sent out will return three times, whether it is positive or negative." This is our commandment.

We believe you create your own reality. And you are responsible for that reality. In essence your life is in your hands. Your luck is the luck you create for yourself.

We have another law: "An it harm none, do what you will." This statement includes self. So as you can see there is a lot to this ancient way. But it is a way of finding your bliss.

I found the craft in the beginning of the '70s, and through it I found my peace. There is much to learn. You will never be bored once you begin practicing Wicca. Once you step on the path it becomes a constant movement of knowledge and understanding. The reason you are on the earth will begin to unfold before you. In time you will understand what your lessons are.

We in the craft believe in more then one god. We believe in the Goddess as well as God. All life comes through her. We honor the Goddess above all things for this reason. In most other religions there is only one God, a male, but not in the craft.

We worship the Goddess and the Horned God, her consort. His horns are of the animal kingdom. All of the animal kingdom is considered divine in addition to people. The Horned God is the lord of death who is the protector of souls. He is the hunter and provider. We don't look upon him as a devil because he has horns. We of the craft don't believe in demons and devils. That is a Christian, Judaic concept. It is not a part of our myths. We worship our gods and goddesses as above us, but we can feel them within us, and about us. We are all one connected by spirit. The gods, goddesses, people, the animal kingdom and all of nature are interconnected. Nothing in the universe is separate. All have impact and affect each other in the most profound way.

When coming from a tradition of only one God you need to submerge yourself in the Goddess to get to know her. Once you do this, you will feel your heart open. The transition is amazing. You need to know the myths. Read as much about them as you can. There are hundreds of books published on mythology. There is so much you can learn about yourself by reading the myths. One of the keys to Wicca is the knowledge of yourself.

Further on in this Book of Shadows I will teach you how to journey with the Gods and Goddesses. When you journey with them you will receive one-on-one instruction from them.

Worshiping the Gods and Goddesses

In most other religions only a male God is worshiped. He is on high, far above us, and he might hear our prayers or not. All you can do is hope for the best. In Wicca, we see the ultimate force as energy, an energy that has no description but contains all the knowledge and love of the universe. Emanating from it are the gods and goddesses. Emanating from the gods and goddesses are men and women. All are inter-connected. Nothing is separate. So our gods and goddesses are within us, and all that is alive. Animals have this same connection with the gods and goddesses as we do. So all are divine because we all contain that spark of energy within us. Our gods and goddesses are within us, above us, beneath us, beside us, behind us and before us. We have a relationship with them that flows easily and comfortably. So we never wonder if they hear us, because we can feel it. Coming from a Catholic background I certainly know the difference.

In EarthGuard we worship the Goddess Gaia because she is one of the oldest goddesses known on earth. Gaia is the earth and she has the greatest influence on us. She feeds us and takes us through our lessons in the physical world. She is the great mother of fertility, prosperity, growth and transformation. We are one in spirit with her, and when our spirits leave earth our bodies become part of her. She contains all the knowledge of the universe. We come to her to learn physical lessons. All who come to the physical world will know her.

We also worship the Goddess Diana. She is the moon goddess that affects the ocean tides and our emotions. Next to the earth, she has the greatest effect on us. When we pray we pray to the moon and the moon goddess. Our emotions govern almost everything we do and the choices we make. Our direction comes from the moon goddess. Our subconscious and conscious thoughts are the basis of all the lessons on earth. She helps us to sort through these lessons and to bring about balance to our choices. We ask for her guidance in spiritual matters, where we ask for guidance from Gaia in all physical matters.

We also worship the great Horned God Herne. He is the great hunter, provider and the guardian of souls. He is the protector and the strength when we need it. He is also of the animal kingdom, so he has the knowledge of the animal world, which is considered divine. We ask his aid when our time of passing comes, and we don't fear him because he, above all, is our protector. These are but names we use for these energies. They are the energies of the spirit of the Earth Mother, the Moon Goddess and the Horned God. If you were to use other names for these goddesses and god, it would not make any difference. It is your intension and visualization that counts.

The Great Oak

There is a great oak that stands on the family hill and all the little trees; they turn to him still.

He teaches them how to plant the seed of love and affection and guides them to grow in an upward direction.

His strong roots feed the soul of their being and give them a sense of pride and a life with more meaning.

Sometimes an act of nature will break a little tree's heart and he'll reach out with his branches, so the healing process can start.

From his warmth and wisdom many little trees have grown and become big oaks and had seedlings of their own.

Often they still look up to him for his wisdom to advise they know he has a powerful mind and answers always wise.

But what the trees don't often say but in their heart it shows, the the oak is honored and lolved much more than he'll ever know.

So I thank you big oak for all to me you gave because I know that when I had fallen it was my life you saved.

By Lady Diana, Path of the Sacred Grove

Chapter 2

Your First Steps On the Path

Discovering Self through the Elements
The Discovery Book

One of the important aspects of the craft is the discovery of self. We utilize the four elements to do this. It's a way to see your strengths and weaknesses. When you can discover this you can make changes in the areas that are lacking and the areas that have too much emphasis. Balance is what we strive for in our lives. If you view the pentagram as yourself, the star within the circle of containment and feel the elements within, you can imagine the feeling of balance. Take some time now before you begin your journey with the discovery book to feel that sense of balance.

We begin by connecting with the earth energies by standing in the star position (see picture overleaf) with your left palm up and your right palm down as shown above. Say out loud three times: "I am one with the earth energies, I can feel it moving throughout my body and connecting with my spirit." Now feel the energy in your left palm, and then the right. When you can feel that energy in your palms it is time to begin your pentagram meditation.

Pentagram Meditation

Find a quiet and comfortable place to sit, close your eyes and begin to breathe deeply. Fill your lungs completely, then hold

Manun, High Priest of the Path of the Sacred Pentagram Grove standing in the star position.

it in for the count of two. Exhale completely holding it out for the count of two. Do this deep breathing exercise for 10 breaths, then develop a comfortable breathing patter for yourself.

Imagine yourself exactly where you are now. Before you appears a human-sized pentagram contained within a circle. In the legs of the star is a place for your feet and legs. At either side in the arms of the star is a place for your arms and hands. At the top is a perfect place for your neck and head. And finally in the center is a place for your body, making a perfect fit just for you. Before you step into place, you walk around it and notice the symbols etched into each point.

At the point where your right hand would fit is an inverted triangle representing the element of water. On the opposite side where your left hand fits is an upright triangle with a line going diagonally through it representing the element of air. Where you will place your right foot is engraved a triangle pointing up, representing the element of fire. And across from it where you will place your left foot is engraved an inverted triangle with a diagonal line going through it, representing the element of earth. At the top point where your head will fit is engraved a wheel with eight spokes, and in the center a crescent moon with its points facing up, representing the spirit. It is time to enter the pentagram.

First step is to put your right hand into place. You can feel a surge of emotional energy the color of clear green going into the tips of your fingers and moving up through your arm, swirling around your heart and settling in your solar plexus. What an amazing feeling. Slowly a ball of energy begins to form in your solar plexus. Place your left hand in the pentagram. You can feel another surge of energy, a brilliant blue going from the tips of the fingers of your left hand, traveling up to the top of your head, swirling around, expanding your thoughts and then settling in your solar plexus. You can see the two brilliant colors of energy swirling around each other increasing the size of the ball in your solar plexus. You can feel the ball of energy building. Now it is time to put your right foot into place, and as you do this you can feel another surge of energy that is a brilliant clear red coming into the arch of your foot, traveling up your leg, swirling around your genital area and settling in the solar plexus. You can see the three colors swirling around forming beautiful energy patterns as it increases the size of the ball of energy there. Now it is time for the final step by placing your left foot in its place along with aligning your body into place. A surge of yellow energy flows into the arch of your left foot, circulating throughout your body and settling in your solar plexus. As the last color enters the ball, all the colors combine forming an incredibly brilliant white light. You can feel the balance of all four elements in your body swirling around to form the ball of energy. The ball of energy now flows up through your neck and head, swirling like a large wheel just above your head. The feeling is like no other. It is the feeling of completeness, of being whole. All is as it should be. This also carries with it the feeling of connection with the universe.

It is time to return to the present. Breathe deeply, filling your lungs completely. You can feel yourself waking up to your environment, slowly becoming aware of this time, this place and this moment. When you are ready you can open your eyes.

Which color stood out more then the others for you? Was there a color that was not as brilliant for you as the other colors? Make note if this happened. This is important to recall. These are clues on the work you need to do in discovering yourself. Whenever you feel out of sorts, this is a good meditation to do. It is time to begin work on yourself. Start by reviewing your week. For instance, if you separate your daily habits and interactions with people into elements, it will become clear to you which elements are predominate in your personality. Take a piece a paper and write on it in columns: Positive Air/Negative Air, Positive Fire/Negative Fire, Positive Water/Negative Water, Positive Earth/Negative Earth. Now recall your week and what interactions took place with other people. How did you performed your jobs or handle different situations? Make a list such as:

Example:

1. Had an argument with Bill the other day.
2. Got my room cleaned up like I wanted.
3. Finished an assignment for work on time.
4. Overate at an all-you-can-eat restaurant.

Results:

1. This would be Negative Fire.
2. Positive Earth.
3. Positive Air.
4. Negative Earth.

You will need a journal to write in. There are rules that go along with doing this kind of journey. In order to be completely honest with yourself, no one should see your journal, not even your mate, if you have one. So have a secret place that is safe from curious eyes. This is a journey you will be taking with yourself, and with it you will be able to see yourself more clearly. We do many things automatically that we might not be aware of. With this journey you will be turning on the light, so to speak. You will have direction on what you need to do to make yourself more successful in your life and in your craft.

You need to take into consideration the meaning behind earth, air, fire and water. In the realm of air we consider knowledge. It is the influence of air that brings in ideas. This is the positive side of air. All planning comes from this realm. Other words associated with air would be: alert, versatile, expressive, cooperative and tolerant. The negative side would be the lack of knowledge, stupidity and ignorance. Also, jumping into something without first looking into it.

Fire is the will behind all things created. The element of fire would be the realm of the will. Other words associated with fire are: freedom, courage, enterprising, creative and taking initiative, pushing forward. Negative fire would be anger unleashed on someone, not considering others when you do something. Letting your will take over your consciousness without reason.

Positive Water is caring about someone else's feelings before you act, not reacting with anger, showing love. Other words associated with water: emotional, compassion, secretive and indulgent. Negative water is losing control of your emotions, not taking a step in a situation when you know you should.

Positive Earth would be completing a project well done, sticking to something even when the odds are against you. Other words associated with earth: practical, possessive, industrious and dependable. Negative Earth would be bragging, gluttony, gossiping and laziness.

How to Begin Your Three-Month Journey

Step 1: Take a journal and divide it into two parts. Only work with the first half of the book to begin with. Each morning when you wake focus your attention on anything in your room, and say a positive affirmation, i.e.: "I'm the happiest person in the world today." Keep the same affirmation throughout your day. Change it each morning, or not. It is up to you. If you find an affirmation that makes a difference in your life, keep it. When you write in your journal, record the affirmation you used. Also, take notice of your energy level upon awakening. Are you ready to start your day or would you rather roll over and sleep? Make a mental note. Then at lunchtime stop whatever you are doing and focus your attention on something around you. Say the positive affirmation. Take note of your energy level. Do it once more at dinnertime and before you retire for the day. Write the highlights of your day. This should only take fifteen minutes at most. The reason you stopped at different times of the day is to give yourself reference points. If I would ask you to recall yesterday, it would take you time to sort through your memory and answer. But if you had times you stopped during your day to make note of how you felt, it would be easy to recall. They are your reference points. Remember to take note of your energy level each time you stop during the day and whether you ate or not, and what you ate. Food can give you energy or deplete energy. This is important to know about yourself. You will learn what food groups affect your energy levels positively and negativity.

Step 1: Write about the things that are significant. Be sure you date each entry. Everyday has something that stands out. It could be how you reacted or not to someone or something, etc. You need to be careful not to overdo this or it will become a chore. Remember the highlights of the day only. If nothing stands out, then write: "Nothing." Occasionally we have those days.

Step 2: At the end of three months you need to review. Reread everything you wrote for the past three months and make a list. Example:

1. Lost my temper;
2. Overslept;
3. Took time to write a letter;
4. Had a good conversation with my boss.

Now if something shows up more than once, don't rewrite it. Put a star or an X next to it.

Step 3: Now it is time to work with the second half of your journal. Separate it into eight parts. Label the sections as you did before, Positive Air, Negative Air, and so on. Simply take your list and fit each thing into its proper element, positive or negative. Once you do this the pictures begin to form. Take note of the longest and shortest lists. What element do you have too much of and what do you have too little of? It will become clear to you what you need to work on to balance your life. Over the years I have journeyed this way many, many times. It's amazing when you pick up a journal you wrote several years before and reread it. You can see your own progress. This keeps a record of your life. Before you make a major step or decision in your life do a discovery journey.

Step 4: Now it is time to make a chart of your energy levels. Here you will learn which day of the week and hour of the day is the most powerful time for you. When you add the phases of the moon to your chart you can see which phase affects you most. By doing this for three months you can also see if there is a pattern.

In your notes you wrote whether or not you ate and what you ate. This will show the effects food has on your body at different times of the day. Does it make you tired or does it give you energy? Your energy chart will pinpoint all of this.

Why is this important? Well, if you are planning to do magickal work of importance, it is best done in the time of day you have the most energy. And you will be able to do the work in the phase of the moon that is most positive for you. You need to know whether you should eat before or not. Some people could go to sleep after a meal while others get more energy after eating. This is just getting to know yourself and how your body works. Go back over the dates and look up the phases of the moon so you can place it on your chart. You might find out that a particular phase works better than another emotionally. I found it easier to make a chart by the week. Then compare three months worth. You will be amazed at the information that is available about yourself that you took for granted.

You will know:

1. Your most powerful time of the day.
2. Your most powerful day of the week.
3. Your most powerful week of the month.
4. The phase of the moon that affects you most, both positively and negatively.

These are the most important things to know about yourself magically to be successful in all that you do. This will change in time. That's why you want to do this at different times of your life. Our lives are changing on a constant basis. Our body needs change periodically. So updates are important. Here on the next page is an example of a week's charting:

Energy Chart Example
Phases of the Moon

Days of the Month
8/11 8/12 8/13 8/14 8/15 8/16 8/17
Days of the week

Hours	Mon	Tues	Wed	Thurs	Fri	Sat	Sun
7am	M	L	M	M	M	M	
8	a						
9				a	a	a	
10							L
11							
12pm	H/a			H	H	M	
1		M/a	H/a				M/a
2							
3	L			M/a	M	L	L
4						a	
5							
6	H/a	M/a	H/a	H/a	H	M	M
7						a	
8							a
9							
10		L	M				
11							
	H			L	H/a	M	M

H-High
M- Medium
L- Low
a- ate

Looking at this chart, which day of the week would be the highest energy day and time of day?

I would say Monday and Friday are the highest energy days, and the time between 6 and 11 p.m. seems to be the most productive. The full moon might have something to do with this. You could only tell this if you had the full three months completed. You then have a clearer picture. This is why three months of data is important to accumulate.

On the next page is an energy chart for you to copy. I would suggest you make enough for three months and put them in a binder for you to work with.

Energy Chart

Phases of the Moon

Days of the Month

Days of the week

Hours	Mon	Tues	Wed	Thurs	Fri	Sat	Sun

Choosing a Magickal Name

In the craft we choose a magickal name. This marks your birth into the craft. When you were born into your family your parents chose your name. In the craft you get to choose a name that has meaning to you. It can be a name from mythology or something in nature. It can be a person whom you admire.

When I first entered the craft I read over many lists of names from Amber to Vivian. There were names like Spring and River, things in nature. There are so many names, it can be difficult to choose.

One of the people in my group told me the unique way he chose his name. He took a set of dice and placed the Rune alphabet on them. The Runes are an ancient Celtic and magickal alphabet. He kept throwing the dice until he was able to put together a name. He did it this way because he felt the Goddess would have a hand in choosing his name. I came across the name of Cara. I liked the sound of it. It's meaning is friend and dear one.

Friendship was very important to me at that time and still is. So it always felt right and still does, more than 30 years later. I have a technique you can use to journey with your name to see if it is the proper magickal name for you. The people I've worked with said it was a great help, so I shall pass it on to you.

Journeying with Your Name

Choose a name from mythology or nature. You must find out the meaning of the name. Sometimes a baby book of names is very helpful. It gives the meaning of the names and their origin. All this information is very important to know. When you choose a name some of its aspects become part of you. Take time researching your name. When you feel you have taken your research as far as you can, then gather things that may be associated with the name. For example, consider the name Amber. It is a beautiful, clear honey-colored resin stone which comes from pine trees. It has qualities of drawing prosperity and healing. It gives you the feeling of having a piece of the sun. Amber will uplift the spirit. It also comes in a soft resin or oil that has a wonderful scent. If I chose this name I would need to incorporate it in my ritual necklace. I would wear some of the oil and then meditate with a pine tree.

I would ask myself: Does it connect me to the Goddess? You might want to see if its numerical value matches with your energies. Here is a chart of the value of the letters. Amber is A 1, m 4, b 2, e 5, and r 9.

Amber = 21

Then take the number to its lowest denominator, which in this case is 3.

1	2	3	4	5	6	7	8	9
a	b	c	d	e	f	g	h	i
j	k	l	m	n	o	p	q	r
s	t	u	v	w	x	y	z	

The number three is creative and expressive. Its life cycle is one of enjoyment and friendships. Its negative side would be jealousy. If you enjoy or need to express yourself more, this is a good name for you. But if you are jealous at heart, then it could cause you some problems. You need to consider all aspects of the name. It will be the name you will use in circle and with all craft-related things. It will be with you for a long time, so take your time when choosing it.

Here are the meanings both positive and negative of the numbers from 1 through 9.

Characteristics of Numbers for Names

Positive	Negative
1. Motivation, center of things	Lack of consideration
2. Sensitive, rhythm, receptivity	Paranoia, super sensitivity
3. Expressive, creative, charm	Conceit, antisocial, jealous
4. Self-discipline, practical, order	Isolation, fixed opinions
5. Freedom, adaptability, adventure	Overindulgence, restlessness
6. Responsible, harmony, healer	Interference, over-anxiety
7. Wisdom, intellect, secrecy	Ignorance, pessimism, chaos
8. Material freedom, control	Greed, strain, abuse
9. Fulfillment, completion	Irresponsibility, bitterness

When you feel you have the right name it is time to take a journey with it. Using the name Amber, I would start by wearing the stone on a necklace. I would put some of the oil on everyday for one month. Amber would be part of my vibration for at least 30 days. I would erect a circle as near to the full moon as possible and place all the things I collected on the altar. I would invoke the Goddess to help aid my work and then go into meditation. I would envision myself holding all the things I gathered for my name. I would then see myself breathing in what I was holding so it would become part of my being. Now I would be able to feel if Amber was right for me.

Choose your name and make it yours. When you go through a dedication to the gods, the name will be yours. Further on you will find a dedication ritual that will be the first door to open you up to the craft.

A Collection of Craft Names, Values and Their Meanings For Women and Men

Women

Name	Pantheon	Numerical Value	Commonly Known for
Aglaia	Greek	4	One of the three Graces/ brilliance
Astraea	Greek	2	Justice
Istar	Semitic	4	Abundance
Aphrodite	Greek	6	Beauty and Love
Athene	Greek	8	Wisdom
Brighid	Gaelic	3	Rivers, Triple Goddess
Blodeuwedd	Welsh	5	Owls, Flowers, beauty
Alcestis	Greek	7	Flowers
Demeter	Greek	7	Protection, abundance
Diana	Roman	2	Moon Goddess, Hunting
Eos	Greek	3	The Dawn
Eostre	Teutonic	1	Earth Goddess
Erzulie	Haitian	9	Goddess of Love
Europa	Greek	4	Beauty
Freya	Norse	1	Youth, Love
Goda	British	9	Beltane Goddess
Hathor	Egyptian	7	Joy, Love
Holda	Teutonic	4	Moon/ Witch Goddess

Horae	Latin	2	Changing of the Seasons
Inanna	Sumerian	8	Queen of Heaven
Lakshmi	Hindu	1	Good Fortune
Morrigan	Pre-Celtic	5	Moon Goddess
Tellus	Roman	8	Purification
Scathach	Irish	9	Warrior Goddess
Venus	Roman	9	Love, Beauty

Men

Name	**Pantheon**	**Numerical Value**	**Meaning**
Ares	Greek	7	War God
Ard-Regh (Ard-Ree)	Irish	7	High King
Athair (Ah-hir)	Irish	3	Father
Annwn	Welsh	3	God of the Underworld
Apollo	Greek	8	Beauty
Bal (Baal)	Mid-Eastern	6	Lord
Bel	Celtic	1	Fire God
Ceird (Kay-erd)	Gaelic	3	Master Smith
Cnoc Sidhe (knock shee)	Irish	8	Hill of Faeries
Cu Chulainn	Irish	7	Irish Hero
Cormac	Irish	8	High King
Dagda (Dag Da)	Irish	8	Father of all Gods
Dulem Reg nan Dul (Dool-em, Ree Nah-in-dool)	Irish	7	King of the Elements

Treadwell's

BOOKSHOP & EVENTS

Who we are and what we're about

Treadwell's was founded in 2003, with the aim of giving London a place for people interested in Western esotericism and worldwide paganism. We offer a friendly open-door policy to the well-known, the infamous and the anonymous alike.

Our books are eclectic, and we are proud of this fact. We cover the quirky aspects of Western culture as well as magic: novels, psychology and travel, as well as grimoires, spell-books and alchemy texts and palmistry tracts. We have Dickens as well as Crowley, Austen as well as Nostradamus. Hopefully somewhere on our shelves is something for every curious mind.

In our main subjects, pagan religions and magic, we have some of the best works available; this is our speciality and our staff are able to offer informed advice. We are here to help, whether you are an artist using mystical symbolism, a journalist doing a story, a student writing a thesis, or simply a naturally inquisitive person. We will try to advise you on the best books for your needs.

Of course you are welcome to let synchronicity choose your books, by just browsing. You can happily meander through our books at your leisure, and leaf through them on our Browser's Sofa. We will never rush you.

By night, we offer lectures, book launches and soirées. Our talks are given by invited researchers as well as by contemporary pagan magicians, and we aim to build bridges between scholars and practitioners, between academic learning and lived experience. Each talk is concluded with a wine and drinks party for all who attend.

Welcome and enjoy!
Christina and all at Treadwell's

Gawain	Celtic	1	Courage
Gwion	Celtic	5	Knowledge
Hercules	Roman	1	God of power
Janus	Roman	2	God of gateways, beginnings
Lleu	Welsh	5	Light
Manannan	Celtic	9	Sea God
Merlin	British	8	Magician, power
Odin	Norse	2	God
Pan	Roman	4	God of the woods, Lust
Qamatha	South Africa	7	Creation God
Tagaloa	Polynesia	3	Ocean God
Tammuz	Mesopotamia	4	Lightning
Tan-Gun	Korea	5	Lord of the sandlewood tree
Taranis	Celtic	1	Thunder, Lightning
Thoth	Egyptian	8	Wisdom
Yggdrasil	Norse	3	World Tree
Yucahu	Caribbean	7	Lord of fertility

When choosing a name you can have more then one, such as Lleu Qamatha, which would take on the meaning of Light God of creation. Its numerical value would then be a 3, instead of 7 and 5. Sometimes when you combine names it changes the numerical value and meaning.

Working with the Tides

You will learn in Wicca to work according to the ocean tides and with the phases of the moon. The tides are the energy flow of growing and resting times of the earth. We work on new things and developing new ideas after Imbolc, also known as Candlemas, February 2. This is when we can see the first signs of life in nature after a long winter's rest. So, too, it is with us. When watching the earth's cycles you will experience the seasons of your life. As the earth changes, so do we. As it grows and is fruitful, so are we. As we harvest what the earth produces for us, so do we harvest what we have accomplished in our lives. This is from Candlemas through Samhain When it goes into its resting season from Samhain through Candlemas, so should we. To do this will bring about harmony.

Working with the Phases of the Moon

Beginning with the first sign of the moon after a new moon is the first phase of the waxing moon. It is when we begin working on the increasing energies. These energies continue until the full of the moon. The most powerful increasing energy is the night before the full, the full moon and the night after. In magickal work, the night before is having a clear picture of the work being done. The full moon is directing that work. The day after is completion of the work. The time from the dark to the full is also known as the waxing time.

From the full to the dark is known as the waning time. This is for decreasing energies. This is the time you work on getting rid of something or removing obstacles from your life. Here is an example: If you were working on increasing love in your life, you would start your work the day of the first phase of the waxing moon. You would complete the work on the full moon. After the full moon you can work on removing any obstacles that might be in your way of receiving that love. As the moon increases in size, so do the energies build. When the moon decreases in size, so do the energies lesson.

We work magick and healing according to the phases of the moon. The moon controls the tides of the oceans. Our bodies are about 73 percent water, so of course the moon has a great effect on us. The new moon phase is when the moon is not visible in the sky, when the shadow of the earth comes between the sun and the moon. We don't usually work at that time unless we are working with the crone, or inner knowledge.

Moon in the Twelve Astrological Signs

Here are other factors that may aid your work. The astrological sign the moon is in at the time of your work has an effect on your success. Having an astrological or witches calendar for the year certainly helps.

* If the moon is in the sign of Capricorn, it works best with careers, or stepping up the ladder at work.

* If the moon is in the sign of Aquarius, the best work is with projects and developing good friendships.

* If the moon is in the sign of Pisces, you would work on anything that has to do with creativity, music or compassion

* If the moon is in Aries, this is a good sign to bring about a swift result.
* If the moon is in Taurus, this sign is best to work for prosperity and material things.

* If the moon is in the sign of Gemini, it would be a great time for communications, especially concerning business.

* If the moon is in Cancer, then fertility, working with the Mother Goddess and anything psychic would flow well.

* If the moon is in Leo, it is good for male fertility, courage, strength and confidence.

* If the moon is in Virgo, then it is best to work on good health and healing. If you need to become organized, this is the sign for that.

* If the moon is in Libra, then it is the best time to work on improving relationships, partnerships and any legal matters.

* If the moon is in Scorpio, this sign works best with anything that has to do with the occult, or if you need to find something a Scorpio moon will help.

* If the moon is in the sign of Sagittarius, then work for anything that has to do with protection on long journeys. This could be a soul's journey or physical journey.

Remember, the more energy you put into something the better your results will be. Plan ahead when doing magickal work. Every step you take toward your work puts it into motion.

Working with the Pentagram in EarthGuard

Over the centuries many spiritual paths have used the Pentagram. In EarthGuard we use it to create balance, to form a protective shield, and to invoke spiritual forces. To create balance we meditate on the star of the pentagram, working with the four elements and spirit. It is a good meditation for the morning when you first wake up. It is always recommended to begin each day balanced with the elements. It's always a good way to end your day for a good night sleep. It's always recommended to meditate before you start ritual. Becoming balanced and centered allows the energies to flow freely.

As a shield of protection, we draw this symbol with our Athame or in our mind in the air before ourselves starting with the circle of containment. First visualize a guardian with a sword and shield standing between you and what you feel is threatening. After completing the circle at the top where you first began, you then begin drawing the star going down towards your left and continuing the star until you finish at the top forming an earth pentagram. This is one complete line as such:

1. begin

Earth Pentagram

This shield is powerful protection when you feel the need arises.

Banishing Earth

1. begin

When you banish this shield you visualize the guardian leaving as you start the circle of containment at the far left bottom corner. Then going around making a complete circle and entering the circle to draw the star from the same place you began. You are moving up from the left lower leg of the pentagram to the top center and continuing until you complete the star at the top. You always banish when you no longer feel threatened. Always thank the guardians for their help when you finish.

There are also the elemental shields that we use in erecting a temple. It is most commonly used at each corner of the circle invoking the four Guardians. When drawing the elemental pentagrams you begin the circle at the appropriate direction such as you see above with the Earth Shield.

The Air pentagram begins at the arm on the right side. The circle is drawn first and then goes into the star by entering the circle where you began. The Fire pentagram shields circle begins at the top then goes around and enters the circle at the top going down to the right instead of the left like the earth pentagram.. Above you can see where the Earth pentagram enters and travels down to the left. The Water pentagram circle begins at the far left side and enters from that same point directed towards the right. There are diagrams of each of the elemental pentagrams further down at the Erecting the Temple. You will notice that each pentagram's opposite, is it's banishing pentagram.

When we invoke Deities with the pentagram we draw the earth pentagram without the circle of containment. This is the pentagram we use when invoking. We cannot contain the Gods but invite them to join us as such:

When we ask them to return to their realms we use a banishing earth pentagram. We use the earth pentagram rather then the other elemental pentagrams because we are inviting them to the earth to lend their aid or witness our rituals.

Chapter 3

Circles Basics

Working in a Sacred Space

We of the craft worship within a circle. Each time we wish to worship the gods and connect with them we create a sacred space. The circle contains the energies we create for worshipping, magick and healing. We can erect a temple anywhere. We are not confined to one area or space. We don't need buildings that require money to keep them going. We worship out in nature and in our homes. This is why we don't ask anyone for money. Most Wiccans don't believe that money should ever pass the palms, as the saying goes. Wicca is a shared religion. Everyone takes the responsibility for the things that are needed for their craft.

Why a circle instead of a square? Most things in nature grow this way, such as trees and plants. Also, the earth and the moon are round, so we are in harmony when we are within a circle. All energies seem to flow this way within our galaxy.

We also call the four elements to add balance to our circle and summon the guardians to add strength and protection. When you worship outdoors you get a sense of being part of your environment. When we in EarthGuard have our circles outdoors we wear street clothes to avoid drawing unwanted attention. Groups I have worked with have been using the local parks for years. We have never had a problem. We just look like a group of people having a party in the park. When we are indoors we wear our robes. It always sets the mood for circle. It is easier to focus on spiritual things if dressing is part of the preparation.

But if you are at a festival run by an organization that has taken everything into consideration for your protection, then its OK to wear robes outside. Robes are always appropriate for indoor work if you don't worship skyclad (naked) in your rites. A sacred space is a temple that is in between the worlds of women, men and the Mighty Ones. It is a place set aside for the purpose of worshiping the Goddess and the Ancient Ones.

Magickal Tools

Here are the basics tools of a Wiccan. You don't need to get everything immediately, but in time you will need to collect them.

Altar - This can be any small table. In time you will want a special altar that is only used for this purpose. You will know it when you see it. In EarthGuard we prefer a round altar, keeping with the energies. It is associated with the element of earth.

Altar Bell - Clear sounding; it is associated with the element of air.

Altar Stone - It has a natural hole running through it. It is a symbol of the Goddess and is connected to the element of earth.

Athame – Double-edged knife with a black wooden handle. This is the most important witch's tool. It is associated with the element of air. This knife should never draw blood. The edge should be dull. You will use this to inscribe your circle if you don't have a sword. It can be used in rituals and spells to direct energy. The blade itself should be a comfortable length for you.

Besom - This is the witch's broom to clean the sacred ritual area. It is associated with the earth element.

Black Scrying Mirror - This is a mirror that is black and can be used to focus on for messages or a glimpse into the future. It is one of the main divination tools a Wiccan uses before doing magick. We always do some sort of divination before working magick so we are sure that it is the correct thing to do. It is usually round, about 7 to 9 inches in diameter. I would consider it in the realm of spirit.

Book of Shadows - This is your book of rituals and recipes. It is the book you record your magickal work in. It is very important to keep a record of all you do along with the date for future work.

Book Stand - This will hold your Book of Shadows on the altar. Your hands need to be free for ritual.

Candlesnuffer - To put out your candles after ritual has been completed.

Candlestick holders with candles - There are four altar candles: two representing the God and Goddess, two representing men and women and the connection between them. The colors for the altar can be any color indicative of the work to be done or the season.

There are four candles corresponding to the four directions. The corner candles are: in the east - blue or yellow for air; in the south - red or orange for fire; in the west - green or blue for water; and in the north - yellow or brown for earth. These are the colors used in EarthGuard. Other traditions may use different colors. If you don't have the colors indicated you can use white - it contains all the colors of the rainbow.

Cauldron - It is black and has three legs. It is used for ritual work and for dancing over at Sabbats. When used for divination it is filled with water. When used for dancing over we build a small fire in it or place a candle in it. It is best known for transformation, fertility and cleansing.

Charcoal -This is for use with incense only. There are small briquettes; don't mistaken them for what is used in a barbecue. These you will find either in a metaphysical bookstore, church store or by mail order.

Compass - This is to mark the directions when situating your altar.

Dishes - You will need four: one each for sea salt, water and sacred oil. One is used as a ritual bowl for your libations if you are working inside. The size is up to you. Whatever fits best on your altar.

Incense – Chosen to fit the work to be done. It is usually made from herbs, resins, woods or barks, flowers and oils. You first want to check which of the above go best with the work at hand.

Lighter or matches - To light the candles and bonfires.

Mortar and pestle - To grind resins and herbs in the making of incense.

Necklace – Made of beads or other natural things, such as shells or seeds. It needs to be 16 to 18 inches long so it fits like a choker to form a complete circle around your neck. If it were longer, it would no longer be a circle. The traditional necklace is made of amber and jet. It can be made of anything natural. It represents the cycle of the soul from life to death to life again, never ending.

Oil - Its use would depend on what you are working on or what ritual you will be performing. Further on you will find a list of oils and formulas you will be able to make to fit all occasions.

Robe - It is usually made of a cotton mix for comfort. In EarthGuard we use different colors for the different levels. Yellow is for level one, discovering self. Brown is for level two, working with inner earth. When working in level three we use green for the earth's vegetation. Level four we wear white for the clarity of the waters of the earth. And finally blue for the fifth level working with the planetary forces.

Sea Salt - This is used for purifying the circle and tools. This is associated with the element of earth/water.

Statue or a representation of the God and the Goddess - On my altar I use three: one each for Gaia, Diana and Herne.

Sword - It is mainly needed when there is a coven. The sword is also associated with the element of air. The style of your sword is of your own choosing. It is used to inscribe the circle and used in certain rituals.

Wand - Made of wood, or a tree branch could be used. It measures the length from the inner part of your arm to the length of your longest finger. The color is either black or natural. It is used to invoke and could also be used to inscribe the circle when it isn't proper to use metal, such as forming a faery circle. It comes under the element of fire.

Wheel of the Seasons - This is a wheel about 10 to 12 inches in diameter. It can be made of branches or a wooden disc. If you make it from branches, you will be able to find them at a hobby shop. They are used for making wreaths. In the center you need to make eight spokes to represent each of the sabbats. I took hemp string and braided the spokes. It looks nice and is easy to construct. I then decorated it with silk greenery. I change decorations according to the season. This is used at sabbats.

Preparing the Area for Circle and Your Altar

Some of the things you will need are: a compass, eight candles, (four for the altar, one for each direction). Have ready for the altar: a dish of sea salt, water, incense appropriate for the work, a representation of the Goddess and the God, a wooden pentacle, athame, sword if you have one, (or you can use your athame), a wand, candle snuffer, sacred oil and lighter.

You can erect a magickal temple wherever you like. It is best to find a quiet place where no one will bother you. Gather from nature the special things of the season to mark your circle and decorate your altar. These can be wildflowers or leaves, vines, branches and stones.

Take a stone and place it in the center of the area you will be working in. Now take a wooden stake and attach a string 4 1/2 feet long to it. Place the stake into the ground at the center stone. A traditional magickal circle is nine feet across. Walk out from the center as far as the cord will take you. Place what you have to mark the circle on the ground as you walk around. Walk marking the circle every couple of feet. By the time you reach the beginning where you placed the first piece you will have a perfect nine-foot circle to work in. Now you will need your compass. Take your compass and mark the directions east, west, north and south. Place the appropriate color candle at each direction. Remove the stake and place your altar over the center stone facing north, the realm of the gods. Below is the altar setup.

Altar Setup

When setting up your altar you will want the energies to be balanced. Start with all four elements being represented. The candles are of the element of fire. Place one in each corner of the top of the altar. The Goddess candle is to the right and the God candle is to the top left. In the picture above, there are four candles. There are two white candles representing the

God and Goddess. The other two white candles represent man and woman. This reminds us of the connection between people and the gods. Anoint the candles with oil before you place them on the altar. Further on in this book I will show you how to do this.

Toward the inside of the God candle is the God statue. And inside of the Goddess candle is the statue of the Goddess. Some prefer one statue of the Goddess on their altar. This is your preference. On the altar above are three, for Goddess Gaia, Goddess Diana and God Herne. In between them is the symbol of earth; the wooden pentacle. Pictured above under the pentacle is a crescent moon boline. It isn't necessary to have a boline on the altar. I have one here because I use it and want this magickal tool to contain the energies of all the magickal work I do. This knife is used for gathering herbs in magick.

Place the incense and incense burner to the left of the altar beneath the God candle. It represents the element of air and fire. Place the bell to the Goddess side, just below the candle. It also falls within the realm of air. Place the sword, (if you have one) to the left of the altar facing north. It comes under the element of air. In the picture above is a sword that was in Gerald Gardner's collection. I purchased it from the Ripley's Museum back in the mid-'80s. It came from his Witchcraft Museum on the Isle of Man in England. Unfortunately this museum closed many years ago. The entire contents of the museum was sold to "Ripley's Believe or Not" company. They had it displayed for many years in their museums. When it lost its popularity they put it all up for sale. I was very lucky to have bought several pieces from the collection.

If you don't have a sword, place your athame in its place. It is also an air tool. The wand, a fire element tool, would go to the right of the altar facing north. It is parallel to the sword or athame. This forms a pyramid. At the bottom center would be the dish of sea salt, (element of water or earth), the sacred oil (earth) and the water (representing the element of water). Leaning against the altar or close by is the besom, the Wiccan's broom. Another handy tool (not pictured above) would be the bookstand that holds your Book of Shadows. Place it in the center behind the altar. It is best to have your hands free when doing ritual. Your altar is now complete. If you wish you can have an altar cloth. The altar cloth should be chosen for the colors of the seasons or the work at hand.

Also in the picture above, to the right and below the Goddess candle is my High Priestess crown. The centerpiece was a Sterling silver belt buckle that belonged to Gerald Gardner and was in the collection. I had a silversmith in the craft make it into my crown.

Candles and their Corresponding Colors

There are different types of candles: paraffin (most common), bayberry (seasonal-winter), and bee's wax (royalty of waxes). Paraffin candles are the most common found in a variety of stores. They are the least expensive and easiest to find. You can find them in every color imaginable.

Bayberry is a natural wax that comes from a bush that has waxy, berry-like fruit. It has a wonderful scent and is great for the winter solstice. It is also good in prosperity spells. Bayberries are seasonal and can be found around the yule holiday, so when they come into their season be sure to get your share.

Last but the best is bee's wax. It comes from the honeycombs made by honeybees. It has an incredible scent that burns in a special way. You can actually see the color of the candle in the glow that is around the flame. They also carry the vibrations of the bees, which is very powerful.

Besides the wax, the colors of the candles you use are very important. Color vibration is a powerful tool to use in your work. Color affects us on a deep level. You can experiment with this. We all have favorite colors we enjoy wearing daily. Try changing to colors you don't ordinarily wear. You will immediately feel the difference. Here is a list of colors and what they are usually used for.

White – The most commonly used for just about everything. If you are unsure of the color to use, choose white. It is for purity, spiritual work and cleansing work. It contains all the colors of the spectrum.

Black – This candle is void of color. It has a variety of uses, such as for getting rid of something. It is great with cleansing rituals. It is also used in funerals, rituals and Samhain. Also for exorcisms, bindings, Saturn rituals and when working with the Crone Aspect.

Orange – This color gives your work a boost, so when doing prosperity work always add orange. It is very good when doing healing work. People forget that a person needs energy to heal. It is also used in harvest festivals. If you are doing work with the planet Mercury or for travel, it is good to use this color.

Yellow – This color is best used for inspiration, inner knowledge, sun magic, spring rituals and working with the earth. It is also good to use this color if you are working healing on someone who is depressed and needs uplift.

Brown – This color is good for abundance, earth rituals, rituals to Goddess Gaia and for grounding.

Red – This color is good for love rituals, fire rituals, purification and harvest rituals. Traditionally it is used for initiations, elevations and oath taking. This color is also used when working with the planet Mars.

Gold – We used this color for sun rituals, wealth, happiness and joy rituals. Also can be used in handfasting rituals.

Silver – It is used in Moon Goddess rituals, working with the feminine side and the tides. Also for handfasting rituals.

Blue – This color is for protection, peace, loyalty and working with the element of air. It is also good when working with the planet Jupiter.

Pink – Good in love rituals, calming the emotions and working with the female side of things.

Green – This is great for healing. It is also good for drawing wealth and prosperity to oneself. When healing a love relationship, I always add green.

Purple – This is working with spirit, the higher self, wisdom and solitude. It is good to use this color when working with the hidden side of yourself.

When doing candle work, you can intensify the energies by combining colors, so don't be afraid of experimenting.

Sabbat Candle Colors

Imbolc/Candlemas - White altar candles and white, red, dark blue/black for the maiden, mother and crone

Spring Equinox - Light green for the altar candles, along with white, black/dark blue representing the dark and light being equal at this time.

Beltane - Altar candles are emerald green or yellow. Also have a dark green representing the Oak King.

Summer Solstice - Altar candles are yellow or gold and one white for the Sun God and black for the dark times to come (winter)

Lammas - Emerald Green for the altar candles.

Mabon/Autumn Equinox - Altar candles are green and orange.

Samhain/Halloween - The altar candles are black and orange.

Yule – Altar candles are dark green and red represents the warmth coming back to the earth.

Anointing your Candles

When anointing your candles, you want to use the oil appropriate for the work at hand. For instance, if you are working on healing, use a healing oil. Or if you are doing an Esbat circle, use the Esbat oil, etc. When in doubt, a combination of frankincense and myrrh oil will always work well. In the section on incenses you will find different herbal oils you can use for this purpose.

If you are working with taper candles, start in the center and massage the candle with the oil, going from the center to the end of the top while visualizing the work to be done. Then turn the candle around and do the same from the center to the bottom, always visualizing the same thing. Take a small amount of oil with your fingertips and visualize your energy binding the candle like a package. Then make the motions as such with your fingertips as if you were tying it, starting at the top to the bottom, and say:

> *"Bound this candle,*
> *As I do see,*

All that I vision,
Shall come to be."

Say it three times and end with: "So mote it be."

If you are working with glass cylinder candles, anoint the top of the candle with the oil, moving in a deasil (clockwise) motion. As you are rubbing the oil into the candle, visualize the work to be done. Then hold the candle between your hands and visualize the work complete, then say the above spell. Take some time in preparing your candles. The success you achieve will depend on the amount of work you put into it.

Anointing oils

Here are recipes you can easily put together. It is best to use a dark-colored bottle to store your oils. Use a dropper when measuring if you are making small amounts of anointing oils. The measurements you see are in parts. A part could be a drop or a spoonful. It depends on how much you need. I like to make at least one-half ounce when I blend mine so it lasts for a while. I don't make too large of a batch because it could become rank. I've had that happen. Oils can be expensive, so I take due care not to waste them.

Some Wiccans like to add herbs to strengthen the vibrations. Some add stones that would be appropriate for the formula. Store your oils in a cool, dark place to keep them fresh.

Altar oil
1 part frankincense
1 part myrrh
1/2 part cedar
1/2 part lavender
3 drops vetiver

Earth oil
2 part sandalwood
1 part honeysuckle
1/2 part patchouli
1/2part tulip

Water oil
2 parts orrisroot
1 part heather
1 part lilac
½ part jasmine
½ part carnation

Fireoil
2 parts dragon blood
1 part orange
1 part hyssop
½ part cedar

Air oil
2 parts almond
1 part lily of the valley
½ part lemon verbena

Dark Moon oil
2 parts hyssop
1 part wormwood
6 drops cinnamon
½ part lavender

Full Moon oil
2 parts rose
1 part chamomile
½ part gardenia
½ part lotus
½ part sandalwood

Gaia oil
2 parts amber
½ part sweet pea
½ part primrose
½ part vervain

Diana Oil
2 parts sandalwood
1 part myrrh
½ part jasmine
1 part water lily
½ part bay

Herne oil
1 part fir
1 part cedar
½part patchouli
½ part rosemary

Maiden Goddess Oil
2 part tea rose
1 part vanilla
$^1/_2$ part sweet pea
$^1/_2$ gardenia

Mother Goddess
2 parts musk
1 part rose
$^1/_2$ vanilla
$^1/_2$patchouli

Crone oil
2 parts sandalwood
1 part frankincense
$^1/_2$ part myrrh
1 part lavender

Wishing Oil
1 part amber
1 part sandalwood
$^1/_2$ part violet
3 drops cinnamon

Green Man oil
2 parts frankincense
1 part fir
1 part cypress
$^1/_2$ part cedar
1 part patchouli

Consecration oil
1 part frankincense
1 part myrrh
$^1/_2$ part cinnamon
1 part lavender

Sabbat Oils

Yule oil
1 part bay laurel
1 part pine
$^1/_2$ part cinnamon
$^1/_2$ part clove

Imbloc/Candlemas
1 part hyssop
$^1/_2$ part clove
1 part cedar
$^1/_2$ part anise

Spring Equinox
2 parts musk
1 part vanilla
1 part dragons blood
1 part lotus
1/2 part sweet pea

Baltane-
2 parts rose
1 part vanilla
1 part lotus

Summer Solstice
1 part orange flower
1 part vanilla
1/2 part lotus
1/2 part lilac

Samhane
2 parts fir
1 part bay
1/2 part cinnamon
1/2 part rosemary
1 part rose geranium

Lammus
2 parts lavender
2 parts chamomile
1 part orris root
1/2 part jasmine

Autumn Equinox
2 parts fir
1 part heliotrope
1/2 part carnation
1 part honeysuckle

Chapter 4

Your First Steps with Ritual

How to Prepare Yourself for Ritual

It is just as important that you are in the right frame of mind for the ritual as taking the time to prepare the area. Before you enter a circle you need to prepare body, mind and spirit.

It is traditional to first take a salt bath. Draw a bath and put into it three pinches of sea salt, hyssop herb and rosemary. The sea salt is for purifying, the hyssop and rosemary are for clearing and protection. I like to make a strong tea with the herbs and pour the tea in the bath through a strainer.

Relax in the salt bath, slowly pouring water over yourself. You need to focus on leaving all problems of the day behind. Think about being with the gods and nature spirits. As you do this you will find yourself relaxing. You are now ready to put your circle necklace on and any other jewelry you consider sacred. If you wear a robe or street clothes, put them on with the thought of preparing for ritual. And you are ready to start.

Earth Balance Meditation

To put your mind and spirit in balance, you first need to go into meditation. In this meditation you will be entering the earth with your consciousness. You will be able to breathe easily as you move through her. Lie on the ground or in front of your altar and close your eyes. Breathe deeply, filling your lungs completely. Hold your breath for a count of two, then exhale completely and wait for another count of two before inhaling again. Do this 10 times, and then develop a comfortable breathing pattern for yourself.

Now imagine lying on the ground in soft, sweet-smelling grass, like a plush carpet. It is in a clearing, in a forest surrounded by trees. The sun is shining and there is a cool breeze. As you breathe you feel yourself becoming heavier and heavier. The deeper you breathe the heavier you feel. Slowly you begin to sink into the earth, becoming part of the mother. You can breathe easily without strain. Take a moment now and feel the different organisms that are living and moving through her.

Now feel yourself going down, deeper and deeper into the center of the earth where the earth is like our sun in the sky. Don't worry, you can't get hurt here, but you can feel the intense energy that keeps our world alive. Allow yourself to experience the sun within. Now feel your heartbeat, and feel the heartbeat of the earth. Feel them coming together as one; feel your body, mind and spirit becoming totally balanced. Take a deep breath. Now it makes you feel lighter.

It is time to return. As you breathe, you feel yourself becoming lighter and lighter. At the same time, you feel yourself coming back to the surface, feeling relaxed, balanced and whole. When you feel yourself back, lying on the soft, green grass, you can open your eyes. You are now ready to begin building your temple.

Creating Your Temple

We begin with clearing the energies of the circle. Go to the far most eastern corner where you have the candle marking that direction. Take your besom and sweep the inside of the circle. Start at the altar to the outer edge of the circle and make one complete turn. Walk widdershins (counterclockwise) around the circle while saying:

Lady Thelema cleansing the circle with the besom.

"Besom, besom, Wiccans broom,
Doth clear this place of dark and doom.
From ancient times to the present day,
Here and now, all is sweep away.
So mote it be."

Declaring the Circle

Go to the front of your altar and close your eyes. Visualize a blue-white light forming a circle where your circle is marked. Open your eyes and ring your bell three times, and say:

"Three is the number thy circle shall be,
Sacred to the Goddess,
So mote it be."

Inscribing the Circle

From your altar, take the sword or athame and go to the east. Place the tip to the ground (if you are using your athame, you just need to point it to the ground as you walk), walking deasil (clockwise) around the circle, ending where you began, (signifying an unbroken circle) saying as you walk:

"*I* (say your craft name),
Take up the sword (or athame),
and inscribe the circle round,
From the powers of old,
From times untold
To form this sacred round,
By earth and water,
Air and fire,
By ocean, lake and sea,
I consecrate this sacred place,
In the names of the ancient Three,
Gaia, Diana and Herne,
So mote it be."

Consecration of Salt

Go back to the front of your altar. Place your bowl of salt on the wooden pentacle. Take your athame, placing the tip into the bowl of salt, and say:

"*Sacred be the salt by the powers of the blade,*
From the steel by which was made,
By the earth, land and sea,
By my will,
So mote it be."

Put the bowl of salt back in its place on the altar.

Consecration of Water

Place the bowl of water on the wooden pentacle. Ring the bell three times. Take the wand and place the tip into the water, and say:

"*Blessed be this water pure,*
From thy power wand is sure,
As pure and clean as rivers flow,
As I do will, with all I know,
So mote it be."

Take three pinches of the consecrated salt and place it in the water and stir three times.

Consecration of Incense

Place your incense on the wooden pentacle. Take your athame and place the tip into the incense, and say:

"*By the desire and the will,*
By the knowledge that's instilled,
By my blade with the power,

I consecrate thee at the Wiccans' hour,
So mote it be."

Consecration of the Fire

Place three pinches of incense on the burning charcoal. As you sprinkle the incense, say:

"No harm or fear can come from thee,
Only pure intensions to the powers that be.
So mote it be."

Blessing and Consecrating the Circle

Take the consecrated water and go to the eastern candle. Begin to sprinkle the circle, going one full turn. Return to the point from which you began. While sprinkling, say:

"I bless and consecrate this hallowed ground,
With heart to heart and hand to hand,
Let the ancient powers return,
Where the Wiccans' fires burn.
So mote it be."

Censing the Circle

Take the incense to the eastern candle and walk around censing the circle one full turn. Say:

"Hear ye ancient gods of might,
Come here to this Wiccans' rite,
In secret glade and Wiccans' lone,
By incense, fire and sacred stone,
All around this sacred site,

Guards us all from evils mite.
So mote it be."

When there are others present, you would welcome them by dipping your index finger into the water and drawing an invoking pentagram on their forehead, saying:

"*Welcome* (persons craft name),
To the place that is between the worlds,
Where magick lives and the Goddess gives."

Calling the Guardians of the Four Directions

Go to the east, and with your athame draw an invoking air pentagram in the air, saying:

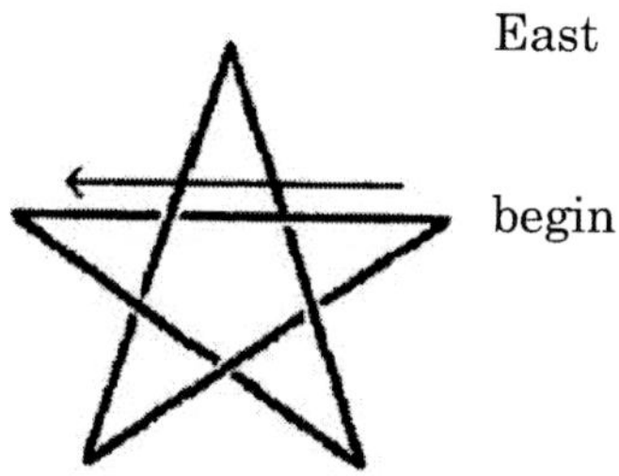

"*In the east the pentagram of air,*
I call upon the power to know,
Let the sword be shown,
And the power be known.
So mote it be."

Salute the direction by raising your athame, kissing the blade and pointing in the direction.

Go to the south and draw an invoking fire pentagram in the air, saying:

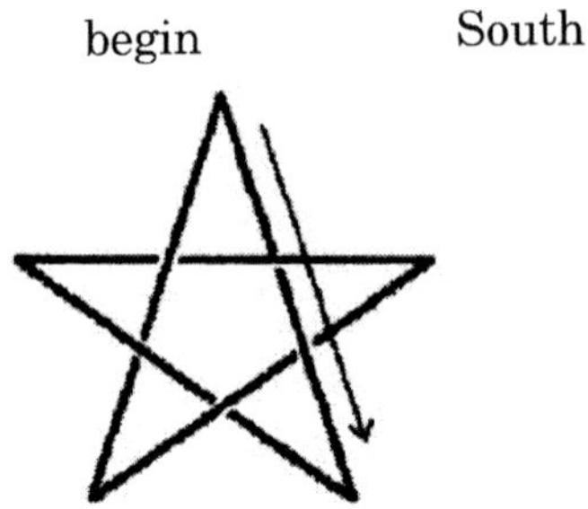

"In the south the pentagram of fire,
I call upon the power of the wand,
Let the wand direct the will,
Let the will direct the desire.
So mote it be."

Salute the direction by raising your athame and kissing the blade. Then point in the direction.

Now go to the west. Draw an invoking water pentagram in the air, saying:

"In the west the pentagram of water,
I call upon the power of the cup,
The chalice of the well,
The cauldron to be filled,
With the emotions that we will.
So mote it be."

Salute the direction with your athame, as done in the other directions.

Go to the north and draw an invoking earth pentagram in the air, saying:

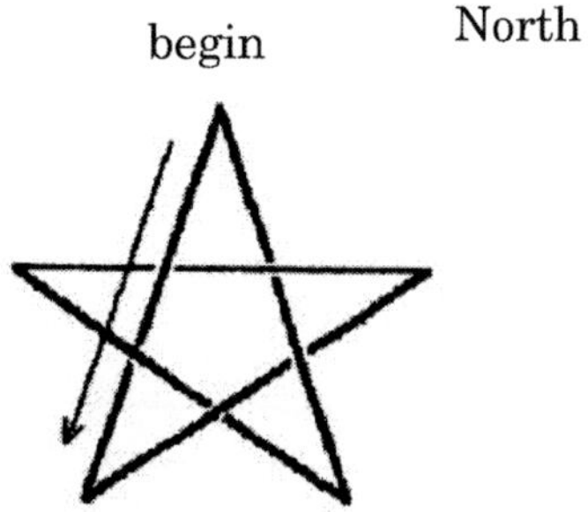

"In the north the pentagram of Earth,
I call upon the power of the pentacle,
The power of silence,
Let the elements entwine,
So the silence shall bind,
All the elements,
Through space and through time.
So mote it be."

Salute the direction in the same manner as you did in the other directions. Return to the front of your altar. It is time to invoke the gods and goddesses to aid your work.

Gaia

Invoking Goddess Gaia

Focus your mind on the beautiful green earth, the forests, mountains, oceans, rivers and lakes. Feel the silent beauty of our mother. When you can see this in your mind and feel what you see, pick up your wooden pentacle and raise it over the altar, and say:

"*By the earth on which we stand,*
By the forest, trees and land,
Beyond all lakes, rivers, and sea,
I invoke thee Gaia,
Earth goddess come unto me,
Blessed be."

Invoking Goddess Diana

Picture in your mind a clear night when in the sky you can see the moon at its fullest. As you gaze upon this moon, you can see slowly forming Goddess Diana, appearing with the crescent moon upon her forehead. As you continue to gaze, you can see her bow-and-arrow, for she is the goddess of the hunt as well as the moon.

When you can see this in your mind, raise your wand and hold it over the altar, saying:

"Oh moon that shines both day and night,
That draws us to this sacred site,
Goddess Diana,
Huntress be,
Fill our circle with tranquility,
Blessed be."

Place the wand back on the altar.

Invoking Horned God Herne

Picture in your mind the lush deep forests where deer run free. You can hear their footsteps as they draw near. You can hear the sound of their antlers as they brush up against tall trees. You can feel the power that is coming closer to you. You can feel the hair on your body begin to stand up as his presence becomes known to you. See this mighty being before you, a male presence with mighty stag horns, a face with dark eyes and strong features. His presence could almost be frightening, but the feeling of being totally protected come over you as he recognizes your presence. When you can see and feel this, raise your sword or athame toward the north, over the altar. Draw an invoking earth pentagram, and say:

"*By the flames burning bright,*
By the day and moonlit night,
In tree groves by forest deep,
Through hidden trails and twisted tree,
We of the craft are drawn to thee,
Here and now at the sacred hour,
We call thee forth to lend your power,
Herne, Herne, Herne,
So mote it be."

You are now ready to do the ritual. It can be an esbat, sabbat, drawing down the moon for a message from the Goddess, or any magickal workings. This also is the time you can do healing or spell work. Further on in this book of shadows you will find different rituals, spells and healing techniques you will be able to master.

After the ritual, it is time to share with the gods and honor them by doing a ritual called Cakes and Wine.

Lady Thelma and Mannun of the Path of the Sacred Pentacle

Ritual of Cakes and Wine

Have on a dish moon cakes or cookies. Have a bottle of wine open. (If you don't wish to have wine, the drink of your choice is fine.) Place the wine on the wooden pentacle and place your hands around the bottle, and say:

"*Sacred be the Goddess' wine we pour,*
Consecrated by ancient lore."

Pour some of the wine in your goblet, and say:

"*As it has been and always will be,*
Blessed by the sacred three,
Gaia, Diana and Herne."

Take your athame and place it in the goblet of wine, and say:

"*Sacred are the symbols of life from thee,*
Contained in all things wild and free."

Pour some of the blessed wine on to the ground if you are outdoors. Or pour some as an offering in a libation bowl to be poured out at a later time.

Place the dish of moon cakes on the wooden pentacle, and with your athame draw an invoking earth pentagram over the cakes, saying:

"*From flour and wheat,*
Milk and honey that's sweet,
Blessings are given each time that we meet.
To the Goddess, blessed be."

Give an offering of the cakes on the ground or in the libation bowl. Eat the cakes and drink the wine. It is important to close the circle when all work is done to return the place to the way it was before your circle. We begin this by taking our wand, holding it over the altar and saying:

"Good pagan folk and faithful friends,
Once more our circle comes to its end,
All work is done and magick complete,
Until once more we merry meet.
So mote it be."

Now turn to the east, and drawing the banishing pentagram for air in that direction while saying:

East

begin

"Take heed, oh guardians of the
Eastern direction,
We thank you for your guidance and protection,
As you leave we hail thee all,
Return once more when we call.
So mote it be."

Complete your circle closing by drawing the appropriate banishing pentagram for each of the directions:

Banishing

South

begin

West

begin

North

begin

Complete the closing by picking up all that marked your circle. Take up the besom and starting in the east walking deasil and sweep the circle, saying:

"*Around once more I sweep thee right,*
Returning all to its natural site.
So mote it be."

Sweep around the area three times. For the circle was drawn three times, once with sword, once with water and once with incense. Your circle is closed.

Chapter 5

Working with Ritual

How to make your own Ritual Salt

Inspired by Perseval

If you are a person who has patience and enjoys crafty things, you will enjoy working with this. All you will need is a gallon of ocean water – or if you live near a saltwater lake, a gallon of it. Place the water in a large ceramic or glass pot, and bring it to boil. Then lower the heat and begin to stir. Continue to stir until all the fluid evaporates. You will be able to see it begin to crystallize as the water goes down. Here is where the patience comes in; this takes at least an hour. The wonderful thing is it makes enough sacred salt for at least a year. While you are stirring, you need to focus on filling it with energy. It is a good thing to say a spell, such as: "I stir beneath stars far brighter, I stir beneath the moon far whiter, charging this salt with power far stronger then even the sun's solar." You can also add herbs to some of it for different rituals or sabbats. It also makes a wonderful coven gift if you visit another group.

How to Consecrate your Tools

On your altar, in addition to what you already have, you need: a cauldron of earth, a bowl of water, a dish of salt, elemental oil and elemental incense to suit the tool. You will also need a white cloth and a black bag or cloth to place the tool into after the consecration.

Tools	Element
Sword/Athame	air
Wand	fire
Wooden pentacle	earth
Bell	air
Besom	earth
Goblet	water
Altar stone	earth
Ritual necklace (Or other ritual jewelry)	earth

Take the tool and place it into the cauldron of earth, and say:

"*Into the cauldron of the crone,*
Transformed, balanced, and be reborn,
So mote it be."

Consecrate the salt and then the water in the usual manner. Place three pinches of salt into the water and stir. Take the bowl of consecrated water and pour it over every part of the tool or jewelry, and say:

"*In the names of the ancient ones of old,*
I consecrate and clean my _______.
As has been done since times untold.
No evil or malice can challenge thee,
Now that it's blessed by the ancient three.
Gaia, Diana and Herne
So mote it be."

Now take the tool and dry it with a white cloth. Sprinkle the incense on the charcoal and put the tool through the smoke three times. Take some of the elemental oil and rub a small amount on every part of the tool. Hold the tool over the altar, and say:

"I invoke the ancient powers to charge my _______.
"O-ee-a,
O-ee-a,
Ee-a-ee-a,
Gaia, Diana and Herne."

Take the tool and use it in the appropriate way to give it its spark. Or if it is jewelry, put it on for the rest of the circle.

Place your consecrated tool in the black bag or wrap it in the black cloth so the energies you want to stay in will, and all unwanted energies will be kept out. When you consecrate the besom, you only need to rub the oil on the handle. The water takes care of the rest.

Dedication to the Gods and Goddesses

Besides what you usually have on the altar, you will need a white candle. This ritual should be done closest to the full moon as possible.

As in times of old when a spiritual path is recognized, a dedication and oath marks the undertaking. When the Goddess' path is chosen, the Goddess has then chosen you to learn and teach the ways of nature. With this path go great responsibilities. To walk the ancient path is to take on the responsibilities of self and growth in all spiritual matters. Begin by reading aloud the pledge of a pagan. If this is being done in a group, then the high priestess will read this if a man is being dedicated, or the high priest if a women is being dedicated.

"Listen well to the pledge of the Goddess.

Know that if it does not ring clear in your (my) heart, then this path is not of your (my) taking. You (I am) are a part of the whole of nature. You (I) know that all the species of the earth are interconnected. And they deserve to be honored, respected and understood. In the ways of nature there is great diversity. You (we) as humans must be tolerant of all species. We (I) must be tolerant of all whose race, appearance, sex, sexual preference, culture and other ways different from our own. We (I) must understand that whatever we (I) send out will return three fold, be it positive or negative. We (I) must take responsibility for all our (my) actions and thoughts. We (I) know and seek to understand that we (I) create my own reality, be it positive or negative.

(Repeat after me)
I, person's surname, do agree of my own free will that all this is true in my heart.
So mote it be."

Ring the bell three times.

Candidate: "*Hear ye, oh ancient Goddess of the earth. Whose beauty and nurturing feeds us on a daily basis, spiritually and physically. Gaia, Earth Mother, accept my dedication into your family.*

Diana Goddess of the moon, huntress of the woods, you who affect the tides and the emotions of the earth and all beings who live upon it, I ask that you accept me into your family.

Herne, mighty horned hunter, guardian of the forests and the stags. You who are the protector and provider, surround me with your protection and guidance. I ask that you accept me into your family.

Gaia, Diana and Herne, I ask for your guidance and protection as I enter this path of knowledge, which has no ending and is eternal. Light my way so that I may recognize that which comes to me of divine source.

So mote it be."

Kneel at the front of your altar and take the oath of a pagan by saying:

(High Priestess/High Priests says: "*Repeat after me.*")

The Oath

"*I*, (use your surname and craft name) *do swear and promise in the names of all my ancestors, and on my honor, do solemnly swear to honor and respect all species of the earth. I also promise to be tolerant of those whose ways differ from my own. I promise to dedicate myself to learning the ways of nature and strive for balance in all things. I understand that I am a part of all nature, and everything I do or say has impact on the whole, knowing that I create my own reality. I take full responsibility for it, be it positive or negative. I believe in the threefold law of retribution, and know all is returned to me three times. I promise to always strive for my highest ideals and to become all that I can be. All this I swear on all that I value, and may I lose all of what I value most if I break this, my solemn oath. So mote it be.*"

"*Let it be known that I, use your surname, take the name of, use your new craft name, for my magickal name to be known by the gods from this day forward.*"

(High Priestess/ High Priest then say: "*Kneel at the sacred altar.*" They then take the sword and tap the candidate on the left shoulder, right shoulder and lastly the left shoulder, and say your new craft name three times. They then say: "*Your name and your word are your bond. So mote it be.*")

Stand and light your candle, and in your own words dedicate yourself. Then blow out your candle. Your breath is part of your life force, and this will give a bit of yourself to it. Keep it for special magick in the future.

Drawing Down the Moon

Lady Diana and Mannun of Path of the Sacred Grove Coven

Stand in the direction of the moon. Take up your wand and draw an invoking earth pentagram in the air over the altar. Outstretch your arms above your head with your fingers pointing in, in the crescent moon position, and say:

"From the flower and from the tree,
From the oceans I call to thee,
Come, oh mother goddess divine,
From my heart through space and time,

Descend into this sacred place,
Into thy priestess with loving grace,
Great mother goddess hear our call,
Speak through her, a message for all.
Blessed be."

Imagine the Goddess entering the priestess or yourself. Let her words come through. Now read "A Charge of a Goddess."

A Charge of a Goddess

"I am the beauty of the green earth,
My life giving blood is the oceans of this land.
My voice can be heard as the winds blow through the trees.
Know that my love is pure as the first snow on a winter's day.
For all things in nature are of my things.
All acts of love are my rituals and the language of my spirit.
I have always been with you. Before there was a you, and you were but a part of me.
I in my loneliness of the one, created you. And you fulfilled my desire to experience love.
For my children are my heart. Know that I am there with each new being as it takes its first breath. I am there as each being releases its last breath. For your breath is my breath. Your life is my life, your love is my love, and love controls it all.
Your worship of me enlightens the love of the universe and increases the bond between all life.
To worship me at my full moon shows me of your devotion and love.
If you have time of trouble, but speak my name and I will be there for you.
For I was there at the beginning and I will be there at the end of all things."

Rituals for the Phases of the Moon

There are times when you need to perform a certain ritual to honor the moon goddess. The Full Moon Ritual is for the full moon phase. This is the time of the Great Mother Goddess. If you have a special need, you would work on it at this time. Then there is the New Moon Ritual for the dark of the moon, when there is no moon visible in the sky. This is the time of the Ancient Crone of Wisdom. This is the time to work on inner knowledge. The energies are most intense at these times.

Full Moon Ritual

Create your temple in the usual manner. Add to your altar white flowers and a white taper candle that was dressed with moon oil. Stand with your arms outstretched and bow to the moon, and say:

"In thy presence I bow to thee,
From my heart, so mote it be."

Light the white candle, and say:

"Goddess of the silvery moon,
Give to us once more a boon,
As of old and days gone passed,
Our love for you shall forever last.
Blessed be."

Close your eyes and whisper what you need to say to the Goddess and wait for an answer.

Then place your goblet on the pentacle and fill it with wine, water or juice. Take your athame and place it in the goblet, saying:

"As it has been from the beginning
And always will be,
The sacred union of the Gods.
So mote it be."

Make a salute to the Goddess with your goblet, holding it up to the moon, and say:

"Blessings on this sacred night,
Lovely Goddess of the light."

Pour some on the earth (or in a libation bowl, if you are indoors) to honor the Goddess, and say:

"Blessed be."

Take a sip. At this time you can do healing work or close the circle.

New Moon Ritual

On a night when there is no moon in the sky, it is the time of meditation and going within. This is the new moon phase. It is the time of endings and new beginnings. It is also a good time to do scrying. At this time have on the altar a black mirror with two white candles, one on each side, that was anointed with psychic oil. Cast your circle in the usual manner. Pick up your wand, hold it over the altar, and say:

"Ancient mother of the dark,
Darksome queen who's left thy mark,
On all who travels thy path of wisdom,
And knows thy powers of transition,
Here I come to call ye forth,
Bring back the knowledge that once was lost,
I ask of you on this night,

To give to me the second sight.
So mote it be."

Kneel in front of the scrying mirror and focus on the center of the mirror. You can either allow a message to come through or ask a question you need an answer to. When you are finished, stand in the star position, which is your feet apart and your arms outstretched to form a star, and say:

"Now at this time of the darkest moon,
When all is black with no hint of you,
We know you are with us to comfort and make anew,
For all has changed and is being reborn,
We are given another chance at the break of dawn.
Blessed be."

Bow and whisper your name. It is time for the ceremony of cakes and wine.

Then complete all with the circle closing.

Esbat Ritual

This is a ritual that you would perform when there isn't a sabbat, a full moon, or dark moon. We perform it to give thanks for all that the gods and goddesses have given us. It is an appreciation ritual.

Have on the altar a piece of paper and a pen to write with. The altar candles should be white, because white is the balance of all color. They should be anointed with the esbath oil.

Open your circle in the usual manner. Take your wand, go to the north, raise your wand, and say:

"Ancient Goddess, horned hunter of the light,
I honor you this sabbat night,
To the earth your blessings given here in above,
Asking only from us to you our love,
From you we learn of our inner power,
Here and now at the magickal hour,
Forever grateful we shall be,
Forever your children.
So mote it be."

Return to the front of the altar and write on your piece of paper what you are grateful for at this time. When you are finished, fold it, place it in the cauldron and watch it burn, and say:

"All this I am grateful for,
All you have taught me forever more.
So mote it be."

It is time for cakes and wine, followed by a special libation of wine to the gods while saying:

"To the gods of ancient lore,
To the knowledge that will endure.
So mote it be."

Close your circle in the usual manner.

Perseval spinning with Morgaine of Grail Keepers Grove

Spinning Power Chant

This chant is to increase power to your magickal working. Move your altar to the far north of the circle. Stand in the center holding your arms out. Focus your eyes on the altar, making this the focal point of attention. Begin to spin slowly and start chanting:

"*Cup and pentacle,*
Wand of fire,
Bring to me what I desire,
Cauldron of knowledge,

Sword of might,
Manifest my will this night."

With each spin, look at the altar so as not to get dizzy. Focus on your image as you chant and spin faster and faster, then drop and see it done. Then say:

"*So mote it be.*"

This can only be properly done with one or two people. When it is done with two, you hold hands and focus on each others' eyes. Pull back to keep tension, with your feet close to the center as you did when you were a child. You and a friend would hold hands and whip each other around, spinning as fast as you could. More then two would slow down the spinning. If you have a group, two would do the spinning while the others stand along the edge of the circle, clapping and chanting to add energies to the work being done.

Chapter 6
Seasonal Rituals

Seasonal Sabbats For Solitary Practitioners and Groups

Seasonal Sabbats

In this section you will find rituals for solitary worship and group worship. The best way to enjoy the solitary rituals is to record the meditations. Find suitable music for each one and make a tape you can turn on at the appropriate time. It will help you visualize it better and make the experience more enjoyable and meaningful.

Major Sabbat

Imbolc. Candlemas

February 2nd

This is a Celtic fire festival. It is the mid-point of the first half of the year. We are half way through the dark side of the year. You are beginning to see the first signs of life after winter. We know that spring is close, and we need to bring back the light.

Imbolc Ritual For a Solitary

At the altar, a wand, Wheel of the Seasons, three candles that represent the three aspects of the Goddess: maiden (white), mother (red) and crone (dark blue). All candles need to be anointed with their appropriate oils of maiden, mother and crone.

Take the wand and hold it above the altar and invoke the Horned God by saying:

"*By the flame that burns so bright,*
By the day and by the night,
In moonlit groves by forest deep,
Through hidden trails and twisted tree,
We of the craft are drawn to thee,
Here and now on Candlemas, at the sabbat hour,
We call thee forth Great Horned God to lend us your power.
So mote it be."

Place the wand back on the altar, and sit. Take three deep breaths. Feel your body relax. Now visualize yourself back in another time. You are out in the woods on a moonlit night. There is drumming and tin flutes playing. People are coming from everywhere. You follow them and join in the dancing. It is all so exciting. They are all dressed in white to represent light, holding candles. When all arrive at the circle they are anointed with oil and welcomed in by the high priestess. She beckons to you and anoints your forehead with sweet oil. She smiles and says:

"*Welcome to the place of the Goddess.*"

There in the center are three women. The first women is dressed in white with flowers in her hair -- she is the maiden aspect. Standing next to her, wearing red with a crown of lighted candles in her hair, is the mother aspect. And the third, dressed in dark blue with a shawl over her head, is the crone aspect. In front of them is a small but deep hole. The high priest puts on his horned helmet and takes up his staff. He walks around the circle, and all bow to honor him. He stops in front of the Goddesse, takes his staff and slowly lowers it into the hole while saying:

"Take heed oh children of the craft,
Once more the mother will give birth to light,
The Sun God."

All cheer in thanks, and all sit on the ground. As you sit, your eyes close and you are taken back to your own circle. When you open your eyes you light the white candle, and say:

"Maiden bright, who represents the beginning of a new cycle,
Prepare now the mother, which will bring forth new light to the earth,
The Sun God."

You now light the red candle, and say:

"Fruitful mother, who gives light back to the earth by giving birth to the Sun God. From this time forward the light will increase and bring fruitfulness. But in time you will grow in understanding by becoming the crone, the ancient wise woman."

Light the dark blue candle, and say:

"Ancient crone, all pass through your cauldron to renew and be reborn, you who went into the quiet time when Gaia slept and renewed herself. Once more the cycle has begun. I prepare now for the turning of the Wheel of the Seasons, for all things in nature will transform."

Take your wheel and turn it three times, and say:

"Blessed be."

Bless your cakes and wine in the usual manner. Pour a libation to the gods and then eat and drink some yourself. It is time to end and close the circle.

Imbolc Ritual For a Group

Four practitioners are needed for this ritual. A hole is dug in the center of the circle. (If held indoors, a cauldron is used.) Three will represent the maiden, mother and crone aspects of the goddess. A male will represent the Horned God. You will need a Wheel of the Sseason, white candle for the maiden, a red candle for the mother aspect and a dark blue candle for the crone. All are anointed with the oil that corresponds with it.

Erect your temple in the usual manner. The high priestess takes up the sword/athame and draws an invoking earth pentagram to the north where the Horned God stands, and says:

"*By the flame that burns so bright,*
By the day and by the night,
In moonlit groves by forest deep,
Through hidden trails and twisted tree,
We of the craft are drawn to thee,
Here and now on Candlemas, at the sabbat hour,
We call thee forth Great Horned God to lend us your power.
So mote it be."

A young maiden with flowers in her hair begins to walk around the circle enticing the God to follow her. She stops in front of the altar next to the mother, who is wearing a crown of candles. Next to her stands the crone, who has a dark blue shawl over her shoulders and is guarding a cauldron.

The god follows her carrying his staff. He walks to the hole in the ground (or the cauldron) and lowers his staff slowly into the hole, saying:

"*Take heed, oh children of the craft, once more the mother will give birth to the light, the Sun God. Once more the cycle begins. Behold, before you the cauldron of rebirth. The Triple*

Goddess who is three but one, youthful innocence, fruitful mother and wise old women. The sun and moon and earth rules them all. The sun, the life force of our universe, the moon that rules the tides of the earth, and the earth who manifest the power of creation. Without them we cannot be."

Maiden speaks:

"I am the maiden spring, the beginning of the cycle. I prepare now the mother, which I will become and bring new life to the earth."

The maiden lights the candles on the crown that the mother is wearing. The mother speaks:

"I am the mother, I give life back to the earth, and to my children I give knowledge. All who would worship me hold the key of truth. To them do I protect and guard. As the wheel of the year turns once again I prepare to understand it all, as I become the crone and guard the cauldron of transformation."

The crone speaks:

"I am the crone, she who guards the cauldron of transformation and renewal. All who come my way will transform and be renewed. As I, too, will be renewed as the maiden, after the quiet time when the earth comes out of her rest and is fruitful once again. Prepare now for the changing of the seasons, for all things in nature will transform."

The crone takes up the wheel of the seasons and goes to the group and begins the passing of the wheel. Each person turns the wheel three times, then passes it to the next person. Each will turn the wheel three times until all have had a chance. The last person brings it back to the altar and hands the wheel to the maiden, who turns it with the mother and then turns to the crone. Together they turn the wheel three times.

The Crone places the wheel back on the altar.

The Crone then calls for the cauldron to be put in place in the north. A small fire is put into the cauldron (or if inside, a candle). Lively dance music or drumming is played, and the mother says:

"*Let the dance of life and light begin.*"

Couples at this time will dance around the circle and jump over the cauldron. Then singles and sometimes groups of three will dance over the cauldron together. All must dance until the fire goes out.

The ritual of cakes and wine is performed, followed by the circle closing. Usually there is a feast to enjoy.

Minor Sabbat

Spring Equinox. March 21st

At this time of the year the dark and the light of the day are in equal balance. The light is now growing in strength. We begin to see the earth growing in beauty. We focus on what we want to grow in our lives. This is the time to take the first steps to bring into your life what you want to accomplish for the year. But first you must identify that. This is the time for you to have a clear picture of your goal. Take the time to work this out. To know is to manifest.

Spring Equinox Ritual For a Solitary

Have on the altar the Wheel of the Seasons. Have ready a wreath of flowers for your head, or greenery if you are a male. Place one black candle and one white candle on the altar. Decorate your circle and altar with spring flowers. Have a cauldron with spring flowers around its edge with a candle in the center.

Take your wand and hold it over the altar and invoke the Horned God:

"By the flame that burns so bright,
By the day and by the night,
In moonlit groves by forest deep,
Through hidden trails and twisted tree,
We of the craft are drawn to thee.
Here and now at the equinox,
when light and darkness meet at sabbat hour,
We call thee forth Herne of the green wood to lend to us your mighty power.
So mote it be."

Light the black candle. Now sit, close your eyes and breathe deeply, filling your lungs completely. Hold it in for the count of two and exhale completely, holding it out for the count of two. Do this for five breaths. Then adapt a comfortable breathing pattern.

Now envision yourself in a beautiful open field with the sun and the moon visible in the sky at the same time. Know that this is the equinox when night and day are equal. The field is filled with beautiful fragrant flowers. The grass is beginning to turn a greener color. You sit and lean against a tree. There in the field you can see the maiden Goddess walking across the field. With each step she takes flowers appear. It almost seems as though her feet are not touching the ground. Her beauty catches the eye of the Horned God who is standing behind a tree in the forest. He smiles as she passes him. He places a lighted cauldron in the center of the field and beckons her to dance with him over the cauldron. They dance with great joy. They look in your direction and call for you to join them in the celebration. You join the dance and feel as though you were in twilight, as if between two worlds. The joy you feel is incredible. A young golden-haired boy comes to join in the fun. He is the light returning. All stop and hold hands over the cauldron as the Goddess speaks:

"I give thanks to the Sun God as he returns to the earth. He brings with him the joy of life and living. He brings laughter and reminds us of the growing time that is finally here after the long winter's rest. Hail, oh beacon of light, who shines on our path so our lessons will be clear and with divine source. Blessed be."

As they take their leave, you return to the tree and sit leaning against it, reflecting. You close your eyes and begin to breathe deeply, and when you open your eyes you find yourself back in your own circle.

Place the wreath of flowers or the greenery on your head. Then light the white candle from the black candle. Put out the black candle, and say:

"Oh, gracious Goddess, maiden pure,
Whose innocence and beauty does ever lure,
Hear my words, I come to thee,
Into my home bestow love and prosperity.
So mote it be."

Place a candle in your cauldron and light it. Put on some lively music and dance, and jump over the cauldron at least three times. When you are finished, take the Wheel of the Seasons and turn it three times, and say:

"As it has been and will always be,
The turning of the seasons.
So mote it be."

Replace the wheel on the altar.

Now is the time for the ritual of cakes and wine. Then close your circle.

Spring Equinox For a Group

On the altar should be the Wheel of the Seasons, a candle to represent the sun. Spring flowers, spring equinox oil and a wreath of flowers for the Sabbat queen. A bowl is prepared with pieces of folded paper in it for the number of women in the group. All are blank but one, which must have a crescent moon drawn on it. This is placed on the altar.

Place a cauldron in the center of the circle with a candle in it. For this ritual you will need a woman to play the Maiden Goddess, a male to play the Horned God, another male to play the Sun God.

All who are standing around in the circle start to clap their hands slowly, rhythmically. The Horned God is standing in the east and the priestess is standing in the west, holding a wand. She invokes him with the wand saying:

"*By the flame that burns so bright,*
By the day and by the night,
In moonlit groves by forest deep,
Through hidden trails and twisted tree,
We of the craft are drawn to thee,
Here and now at the equinox,
When light and darkness meet at Sabbat hour,
We call thee forth Herne of the green wood,
To lend to us your mighty power.
So mote it be."

The high priestess then walks to the Horned God, kisses him and hands him the wand. She then joins the rest of the group in the circle. The Horned God lights the candle in the cauldron and joins the group. All begin to clap their hands in a slow, rhythmic beat. The Maiden Goddess steps out, as does the Sun God, and does a slow dance around the circle three times. Her dance is enticing. They then come together and hold hands and jump the cauldron together. Then the maiden says:

"I thank the sun for returning once again, bringing with him the power to grow to the earth. All hail the Sun God." All call out, "Hail, oh sun."

Lively music or drumming begins and the maiden and the Sun God lead the group in a cauldron dance. All dance around the circle and jump over the cauldron. When the flame goes out in the cauldron, the dance is done. All return to their places around the circle. The high priest then walks around to all the women with the bowl that has the folded papers in it. The woman who chooses the paper with the crescent moon is crowned Queen of the Sabbat. She will be crowned with flowers and anointed with the spring equinox oil on the forehead (invoking an earth pentagram). All men in the group file by her and give a bow and a kiss on the cheek to honor her. Her job will be to help prepare for the Beltane celebration to come. She will perform the rite of cakes and wine with the male of her choosing.

Then there is the closing of the circle followed by a grand feast.

Major Sabbat

Beltane. May Eve. April 30th

The earth is in full bloom. The signs of the Goddess are everywhere. Fields are being planted. The sun is getting stronger.

Beltane is a fire festival. Tradition in ancient times was to build bonfires on hilltops to celebrate the earth coming to life again. Today a cauldron fire or a campfire works well for most. It is your intent that counts. This marks the beginning of summer in the ancient way of thinking, the growing time for the earth. And it is the earth coming to life in its fullness. The Horned God and the Great Mother Goddess mate to bring forth the fullness of the earth. This is the time of fertility, manifesting what you want to the fullest degree.

Beltane Ritual For a Solitary

You will need a Maypole, which can be any pole that is at least a foot taller then yourself. On top attach a wreath of flowers. To the wreath you will need to attach a white ribbon to represent the Maiden Goddess, red ribbon to represent love, passion and the Mother Goddess, and a dark blue ribbon to represent the ancient Crone of Wisdom. A green ribbon is good to add for healing, good health and prosperity. Then add an orange ribbon for vitality, a brown ribbon for the Horned God and a yellow ribbon for new beginnings. Place your Maypole to the north of your altar. Be sure the ribbons are touching the ground. The wreath represents the Goddess as the pole represents the Horned God. Once in place, it is a breathtaking site.

Place a cauldron with a small fire or a candle to the south of your circle. For your libation, set a goblet of mead, wine, juice or water. The cakes or cookies should be moon cakes, but your favorite cake will be just fine. Have a wreath for your head of greenery if you are a male, or flowers if you are a female.

For the cauldron dance, be sure you have a clear vision of what you want to draw to you. It has been known to draw a husband or a wife; it can cause fertility to come about; for a pregnant woman to bring about an easy birth; or to bring prosperity to your home.

Have a green candle in the center of your altar to represent the Oak King. Your altar candles should be green or yellow. Decorate your altar with seasonal things that may come from your backyard or a park. You may want to place some fresh vegetables, fruits and flowers around the circle. Your altar and circle should look very festive. A green robe is appropriate for the season. But all colors, except black, are good. That is reserved for Samhain or funerals.

Erect your temple in the usual manner. Begin by ringing the bell three times. Light your altar candles and say:

"*By fire and flame,*
By will and by might,
I celebrate the earth,
This Beltane night.
So mote it be."

Place the wreath on your head. Pick up your wand and bless the mead and cakes. Do this by drawing an invoking an earth pentagram over the cakes and wine. Sprinkle some of the wine over the cakes, and say:

"*Blessed be the fruitfulness,*
Of the earth,
Blessed be the union of the gods,
Who has taught us to mirth,
Blessings be upon these cakes and wine,
Honoring the fullness of this Beltane time.
So mote it be."

Take some cake and wine and make a libation to the ground or in the libation bowl, saying:

"*To the gods,*
To the earth,
To the animals,
And to all humans,
All are blessed.
So mote it be."

Take a sip of wine and eat a piece of cake. Sit and lean against the altar and close your eyes. Breathe deeply, relaxing your body and developing a comfortable breathing pattern.

Feel yourself walking on a path in a forest. It is a beautiful day. The sun is bright, but there is a cool breeze. You begin to hear other people in the woods and music off in the distance. Some are carrying huge baskets of food of every kind. You can smell the fresh baked goods. The music is getting louder and there are a lot more people coming from every direction. You stop one of them and ask where they are going. With a big smile they say, "We are off to the sabbat, come join us. All are welcome at Beltane." One of them puts a basket of food in your arms to carry. You smile, feeling very welcome.

The music is getting closer and closer. The energy is getting high. You don't know where you are going, but that doesn't matter. You take a deep breath, give a leap of faith and follow. There in a clearing is a large earth mound with tons of firewood ready to be ignited. Off in the distance is another bonfire being readied on a hilltop close by. That is the main fire. No one can light his or her fire until this fire is lighted. You can see people coming from every direction. It is so exciting. Everyone is waiting for the high priestess to light the hilltop fire to start the festivities. Finally she stands with the torch in her hand to light the Beltane fire. She lights it as the people cheer, then they begin to dance. Two by two, they jump over the bonfire. One of the people comes, grabs you by the hand, and away you go over the fire. Your heart is pounding with delight.

The older women are setting a great feast when suddenly a horn is blown. The high priestess joins the high priest at the altar, and he crowns her with a wreath of wildflowers. A group of men and women begin to sing a soft romantic song of the mating of the God and Goddess. The high priest and priestess begin their dance of love around the circle. It is so beautiful it touches your heart. They disappear into the forest and soon other couples do the same. Those who remain pick up the ribbons and dance around the Maypole. Half of the people are dancing deasil (clockwise) and the others are dancing widdershins (counterclockwise) interweaving ribbons as they go. You go over to the feast and take a sip of mead and once more sit and rest against a nearby tree. You close your eyes and take a deep breath. As you open your eyes you find yourself back in your own circle.

Ring the bell eight times and light the candle that represents the Oak King, and say:

"Hail unto thee, oh mighty Oak King who lives thy life for the love of the Goddess, Blessed be the Summer Goddess who brings forth the fruit of the land so we may live to see another year. So mote it be."

Put on some lively music and light the fire in the cauldron with the Oak King's candle. Dance around the circle three times, each time jumping over the cauldron. Visualize what you want in your life.

Change your music to a lighter dance tune. Walk to the Maypole. Pick up half of the ribbons and dance deasil around the pole three times, once again visualizing your dream. Then pick up the second half and do the same while dancing widdershins, maintaining your vision. Tie off the ribbons in a large knot, and say:

"I am blessed by the Goddess this Beltane day,
All that I worked for is on its way.
So mote it be."

It is time to close the circle and enjoy your feast.

Beltane Ritual For a Group

The altar and circle are decorated with fresh flowers, fruits and vegetables. Have a wreath of flowers on the altar for the crowning of the high priestess. The altar candles are green or yellow. Have a Maypole as tall as the area can accommodate. It will be placed in the north. Usually the men use a tall slender tree, or it could be a pole made of PC piping painted brown or green. Every year the people I worship with have a 27-foot pole that we use in an open field. There are about 80 to 100 of us each year.

The women make the large wreath of greenery and flowers. We go into the woods and pick leafy vines and bendable branches that are on the ground. We use wildflowers to decorate it. Its beauty always amazes me. Both the pole and the wreath are consecrated with sacred wine. The high priest and the men consecrate the pole by calling upon the Horned God to lend his energies to the pole. Then they spill sacred wine on it.

The women and the high priestess consecrate the wreath as they decorate it by sprinkling sacred wine on it and chanting:

"*We honor the Goddess,*
We honor the wreath,
All life comes through her,
This is our belief."

The men and the women come together with the pole and the wreath. The women attach the wreath to the top and the men stand it in place. All is ready for the dance.

A cauldron is placed in the south with wood for a small fire or a candle. One must focus on a vision for the cauldron dance. Some jump the cauldron for fertility, some for prosperity, some to meet the right mate. The vision is yours so choose well.

The high priestess and the high priest erect the temple in the usual manner. They then invite all to join in the celebration of Beltane. The high priestess anoints all the men with Beltane oil. She draws an invoking earth pentagram on their forehead and kisses them on the cheek and says, "Blessed be." The high priest anoints the women in the same way.

Afterwards, there is drumming. The high priest puts on his horned helmet and begins the chase. The high priestess slowly and seductively lets him chase her. But the women of the coven block him just as he is about to catch her. She still entices him to follow, and after three times around the circle she allows him to catch her. The drumming stops and the high priest takes the wreath from the altar and crowns her. At this time a romantic dance follows as the high priest and the high priestess lead all to the Maypole.

Everyone takes a ribbon. Every other person turns to face the person to their right as they await the music to begin. When the dance begins each person moves in and out of each other. Some are putting their ribbons over the next person's head while the next goes under the ribbon. As they dance they form the weaving of the ribbons over the Maypole. This lasts until the ribbons are completely used up. Each person then ties off his or her ribbon. The high priestess takes the Oak King's candle and lights it from the altar candle, and says:

"Hail unto thee, oh mighty Oak King who lives thy life for the love of the Goddess, Blessed be the Summer Goddess who brings forth the fruit of the land so we may live to see another year. So mote it be."

She then lights the fire in the cauldron with his candle and calls out:

"Let the dance of transformation begin."

She takes the high priest's hand and jumps the cauldron. All follow jumping with excitement until the fire goes out, (or is put out). The ritual of cakes and wine follows the dance. Then the circle closing is done in the usual manner. A great feast follows with lots of merriment.

Minor Sabbat

Summer Solstice - June 22nd

This is the longest day of the year. The earth is abundant. It is also the turning point of the year, as after today the days will begin to get shorter. So here is where the God of Light, or the Oak King, (waxing year) falls to the power of the dark side of the year, the Holly King (waning year) as we begin our journey into the second half of the year with his guidance. Remember that the Goddess stays the same. She never dies and needs rebirth. But she goes through her phases of transformation from maiden to mother to crone.

Summer Solstice Ritual For a Solitary

Decorate your altar and circle with summer flowers and leaves. Have on the altar a white candle to represent the sun, the Oak King. You will need a black candle to represent the winter to come and the Holly King. Have a dish of honey and a cup of milk to give a libation of thanks for what the earth has given to us.

A cauldron is set to the west with firewood or a candle ready to be ignited. The Wheel of the Seasons is on the altar decorated half with flowers and half with leaves. Erect your temple in the usual manner. Begin the ritual by ringing the bell three times, and say:

"Hail to the sun which has reached its zenith in the sky,
Hail to the richness of the earth who will once more turn its tide."

Light the Oak King's candle and walk around the circle three times with it to represent the movement of the year. Come back to the front of the altar. Take the honey and pour some on the ground, or if you are indoors pour some in the libation bowl, and say:

"*The earth is abundantly filled,*
I give thanks for all to the Great Mother, this is my will."

Pour some milk on the earth or in the libation bowl, and say:

"*To the gods and goddesses and the powers that be,*
All is fulfilled.
So mote it be."

Sit in front of your altar, close your eyes and breathe deeply, relaxing your body. Imagine yourself walking through the woods on a sunny day. There is a soft warm breeze with the fragrance of wildflowers of summer. As you come out in a clearing you notice a circle of people standing around a stone altar. They gestured for you to join them. The high priestess starts to chant, and all join in chanting:

"*Oak King, Oak King,*
Summers on the rise
Holly King, Holly King,
Come and take your prize."

Then from out of the woods comes a tall man with a wreath of Oak Leaves on his head. He is carrying his staff, walking deasil around the outside of the circle. To the west comes another man with a wreath of holly leaves on his head. He also carries a staff. He sees the Oak King and stops and challenges him. The Holly King and the Oak King battle with their staffs until the Oak King falls to the ground defeated. The high priestess goes to him and throws her shawl over the Oak King, and says:

"The Oak King is dead. The Holly King shall lead us into the dark time of the year with strength. All hail the Holly King."

Everyone cheers.

A beautiful wreath of flowers and leaves is taken off the altar, and each person turns it three times. They hand it to you and gesture for you to do the same. You feel as if you had something to do with the earth's changing its season just by turning the wreath. It is an amazing feeling. You hand it back, and the priestess places it on the altar, and says,

"As it has been done and will always be done for all times.
So mote it be."

The high priest picks up a large cauldron and places it in the center. Other men join him in lighting it. The others begin clapping their hands rhythmically. Two by two they begin to jump over the cauldron as all dance around the circle. One of the people grabs your hand and leads you in a dance, then over the cauldron you go.

Some of the women are setting a feast, and the aromas of the freshly baked breads and dishes of the season are so enticing. They invite you to join them, and you take a slice of warm fruit bread and sit under a beautiful oak tree. As you lean against it you look up to see that it is decorated with colorful ribbons. You begin to feel tired, so you close your eyes for a short rest. As you open your eyes again, you find yourself back in your own circle.

Light the black candle with the white candle to represent the changing of power. Now blow out the white candle to represent the death of the Oak King, and say:

"The Oak King is dead,
But shall be reborn through the Great Mother,

As the earth changes the Holly King is all powerful.
He will guide us through the dark times to come,
I hail thee Holly King."

Light the fire or candle in the cauldron. Put on some lively dance music and dance around the circle remembering the dance you just did with the person from another time. Jump over the cauldron at least three times, feeling the freedom of being yourself. It is time for a circle closing followed by a feast of your favorite foods.

Summer Solstice For a Group

Decorate your altar with flowers and greenery. It is appropriate to have as your altar candles one white taper and one black taper. This represents the changing of the tides. Your Wheel of the Seasons should be decorated with flowers on one half and leaves on the other half. One of the women of the group shall play the maiden. She needs a cloth large enough to cover a man. You will need two men, one to represent the Oak King for the waxing year and one to play the Holly King for the waning year. They should be dressed to reflect this. A cauldron is made ready with firewood or a candle and set to the west.

The circle is opened in the usual manner. The high priestess rings the altar bell four times, stops and rings it four times again. She then lights the white altar candle, and says:

"*The sun is at its zenith, the world is full of light,*
The world is filled of wonder with hope and pure delight."

The high priest lights the black candle, and says:

"The tides are now changing, once more the wheel is turning,
The sun is brightly burning, but soon lesser then before."

Then from the south comes the Oak King walking deasil around the circle with his staff. From the north comes the Holly King walking with his staff widdershins around the circle. He stops in the center. The Holly King challenges the Oak King. The mock battle begins, and the Holly King wins. The Oak King drops to the ground. A maiden of the group takes the cloth and covers the Oak King, and says:

"*The Oak King is dead, The Oak King is dead,*
I fear the light leaving, my heart is so grieving."

The high priestess says:

"*Fear not for he will be reborn,*
Grieve not for the light returns,
Through the Great Mother,
The Sun God is reborn each year.
In peace and joy without tears,
and without fear.
"*So mote it be.*"

The High Priest proclaims:

"*All hail the Holly King,*
All hail what he brings,
He leads us through the darkness of the year,
With strength and protection and without fear,
Hail, Holly King."

All reply:

"*Hail, Holly King.*"

The priestess walks once around the circle with the Holly King and stops at the cauldron. The Holly King lights the cauldron, and with the high priestess starts the cauldron dance. All follow, jumping over the cauldron. The ritual of cakes and wine is performed after the dance. The high priestess takes the Wheel of the Seasons from the altar, and says:

"The tides are now changing, once more the wheel is turning, The sun is brightly burning, but soon lesser then before."

The high priestess turns the wheel three times and passes it deasil to the person next to her as each person turns the wheel three times.

A circle closing is performed, and then all enjoy a great feast.

Major Sabbat

Lughnasadh - August 1st

This is a harvest festival. This is a time of great joy and celebration. A time to give thanks for all the good the earth has given you. For us of the Wiccan faith, we acknowledge the universe, the earth and nature as part of ourselves. It is also a corn festival and in myths the time of the sacrifice of the corn king so the earth will keep giving and replenishing.

Lammas Sabbat For a Solitary

Have on the altar ears of corn, some open showing the yellow kernels. With the husks of the corn make a wreath for your head. Make a corn dolly for the sacrifice by tying together two pieces of cornhusk in the shape of a cross. Split in half the bottom piece for legs and fold down the top piece in half and tie with a cord to make the head. Then place it on the center of the altar. Place one earn of corn at each direction. The Wheel of the Seasons should be decorated with cornhusks and yellow flowers. Have the seasonal flowers on the altar and around the circle. It is appropriate to have a loaf of cornbread on the altar. A cauldron is placed in the center of the circle with wood for a fire or a candle. Have lively dance music ready.

Begin your ritual by ringing the bell three times, and say:

"*Lammas, Lammas, Lammas,*
The earth is bountiful,
The wildlife is joyful,
And I am grateful.
So mote it be."

Put on the music and dance around the circle three times; skipping, jumping, twisting and turning. Fill yourself with the joy of being. At the end of the dance light the cauldron.

Sit in a comfortable position in front of the altar. Breathe deeply, clearing your mind and relaxing your body. It feels good to rest after the dance.

Visualize yourself walking through the woods, when suddenly people are passing you by, saying: "See you at the sabbat, hurry you don't want to be late." You begin to quicken your pace following the others. Suddenly you can hear music playing and people talking as they gather in a large clearing with a fire pit in the center. Some of the men are building the fire while some of the women are making wreaths out of cornhusks with flowers for everyone to wear. Great baskets of food are carried into the clearing. It has been a great harvest. The food is placed on blankets around the outside of the circle. You are asked to help, and as you try they can see you are unsure of yourself. "Here, let me show you," someone says, lending you a hand. They are a friendly bunch, making you feel like a member of the group.

A horn blows, letting everyone know it is time for the ceremony to begin.

There is a young man sitting in a special seat. All the young village women are tending to him. He represents the Corn King. He will make the sacrifice for all so that the year's harvest will be the best, and everyone will benefit. The high priest and priestess open the circle for everyone to enter. Together they bless the food and take the best of each basket for the offering. All in turn take a vegetable or fruit to offer to the Goddess for her generosity. The high priestess kneels in front of the altar as the high priest places the wreath upon her head. Everyone takes their place around the edge of the circle. They begin to clap in a slow, rhythmic way. The high priestess begins her dance, beckoning the Corn King to join her. As he tries to get close, she moves away and laughs. She is enticing him to catch her. Around the circle the chase goes on until finally he catches her, and they embrace. She takes her goblet and holds it out to him. He pours mead into it. He then takes his athame and holds the knife over the goblet, slowly lowering it into her goblet as he says: "God, Goddess come together in peace, love and fruitfulness." He pours some onto the ground in libation to the gods and then offers his high priestess a sip. He then joins her by taking a sip, and says: "Hail the sacred union, So mote it be." All cry out, "Hail and blessed be."

The Corn King takes the corn dolly and walks to the fire. He holds up the corn dolly and says: "In ancient times I gave my blood for the life of the land. I now offer this representation of myself, knowing that all life is sacred to the Goddess." He throws the dolly into the fire, and all cheer him. The drummers begin a lively beat. Everyone follows the Corn King's example by throwing a vegetable into the fire as they begin to dance with great joy around the circle and jump over the fire. The dancing goes on and on. You join in the dance until you drop from exhaustion. You go and sit down to watch the others while trying to catch your breath. You are tired, so you close your eyes for a moment. When you open them, you find yourself back in your own circle.

Stand and place the wreath upon your head. Take the corn dolly and go to the cauldron, holding it up, and say:

"Far from the mountains cold,
Deep in the forests old,
Far back as the mind was told,
This sacrifice ensured our crops,
and filled thy promise foretold.
Blessed be."

Drop the corn dolly into the lighted cauldron. Now pour some wine into your goblet. Take your athame and place it into the wine, and say:

"In the names of the ancient three, I bless and consecrate thee, so mote it be."

Pour some wine as a libation and take a piece of the cornbread. Take a sip of wine and eat the cornbread in honor of the celebration. Put on some lively music and dance around the circle, jumping over the cauldron each time you go around. When you have gone around three times, end by saying, "So mote it be." Do the circle closing and enjoy your feast.

Lammas Sabbat for a Group

Preparation for this sabbat can be fun with a group. Have each person bring an ear of corn. Remove some of the husk and have each person make their own corn dolly. An easy way is described in the ritual for a solitary. Then with the remaining husks have everyone make a wreath for their head. The woman can add flowers to theirs. On the altar you will need the Wheel of the Seasons decorated with some of the cornhusks and flowers. One of the men will be needed to play the part of the Corn King. The best way to choose is with straws: The shortest straw drawn plays the Corn King.

The ritual begins with the ringing of the bell nine times. The high priestess kneels in front of the high priest, and he places the wreath upon her head and helps her up. All follow and put their wreaths on. Slow, rhythmic music is played - or if there are drummers, they play their drums in this manner. The high priestess begins the spiral dance, holding an ear of corn. She ends in the center with everyone spiraled around her. She holds up the corn, then leads the dance out of the coil and back out a circle. She says:

"*The king has been chosen,*
The sacrifice will be met,
All is as it should be,
Before the day's sunset."

The man who has been chosen as the Corn King steps forward, holding a corn dolly. He walks once around about the circle, holding up the corn dolly for all to see. He walks over to the ritual fire (or cauldron), and says:

"*In ancient times I gave my blood for the life of the land. I now offer this representation of myself, knowing that all life is sacred to the Goddess. So mote it be.*"

The Corn King then throws his corn dolly into the fire, and says:

"*Far from the mountains cold,*
Deep in the forests old,
Far back as the mind was told,
This sacrifice ensured our crops,
And filled thy promise foretold.
Blessed be."

All respond: "*Blessed be.*"

The Corn King then beckons everyone to do the same, and all throw their corn dolly into the fire.

The high priest calls out: "*All hail to the Corn King*."

All respond: "*Blessed be and hail to thee*."

Lively music is played, or the drummers play a lively dance beat. The high priestess calls out: "*Let the dance of life begin*." The high priest takes her hand and they start the dancing by jumping over the cauldron. All follow with great joy and merriment. When the dance has ended, the high priestess and the high priest perform the cakes and wine ceremony.

All is then shared with the group. The high priestess removes the Wheel of the Seasons from the altar, and with the high priest, turns it three times. It is then moved from one person to the next until all have turned the wheel. The high priestess replaces it on the altar.

The high priestess holds up her athame, and says:

"*Good pagan folk and faithful friends,*
Once more our sabbat comes to its end,
All work is done and magick is complete,
Until once more we merry meet.
So mote it be."

All respond: " *So Mote It Be*." A circle closing is done.

The high priest says:

"*The circle is open but never broken,*
Merry meet and merry part, and merry meet again."

All respond: "*Merry meet, merry part and merry meet again*."

Everyone embraces and says, "*Blessed be*." The feast begins.

Minor Sabbat

Mabon/Autumn Equinox - September 21

The harvest is plentiful at this time of year. It is a time of joy and celebration. It is a time to recognize what you are harvesting in your life as well as the earth's bounty. It is a cross quarter time for the earth when the day and night are equal.

Mabon/Autumn Equinox For a Solitary

Decorate your sacred space and altar with the foliage in your area. Your circle and altar should have fresh flowers, vegetables and fruits of the season around and on it. Your altar and ritual area should be as colorful as possible. It is appropriate to use green and orange candles for the altar. Place the Wheel of the Seasons on the altar decorated with red, orange, green and yellow ribbons. You will need a piece of paper and a pen. The cauldron should be lighted ahead of time so a fire is going well for the ritual. You will need an ear of corn, a potato cut into small pieces, cornhusks, fresh rosemary herb, dill herb and cord.

Erect your circle in the usual manner, announcing to each corner at the end:

"*And the celebration of our mother's harvest.*"

Begin by ringing the bell three times. Then say:

"*I hail the harvest, for the great mother is plentiful.*"

Ring the bell again three times, and say:

"*I give thanks for all my blessings, physical and non-physical. So mote it be.*"

An ear of corn and a potato are prepared for the fire with fresh rosemary herb and dill. The herbs are for prosperity and protection. Both are wrapped in cornhusk and tied with cord. Foil should be wrapped around them before they are put into the fire to keep them from getting ruined. Take your bell and ring it seven times. With your athame draw an invoking earth pentagram over the corn and potato, and say:

"*Blessings be upon this food born of the mother's womb,*
From beneath the earth and above the earth,
All is sacred to me, blessed be."

The corn and potato are then placed in the cauldron to cook during the ritual. If you are indoors, after the blessing place the corn and potato in your oven to cook during your ritual. This is also a time of weeding out, a time to reflect on what needs to be changed in your own life. Take a moment to think about this. Write on the paper what you need to rid yourself of. Then fold it three times. If you are outdoors, dig a hole and bury it in the earth, and say:

"*Down into the earth you must go,*
Deep into the mother who transforms I know,
That which was wrong make right,
All in my life once more is bright.
So mote it be."

If you are indoors, put your paper aside until you can do this outdoors. Take the Wheel of the Seasons and turn it three times, and say:

"*I turn this wheel of the seasons just as the earth begins another change.*
The earth is forever turning, forever changing. So it is true of the earth,
So it is true of me.
So mote it be."

Put on some lively dance music and dance around the circle three times, jumping over the cauldron each turn. Go back to the altar and perform the cakes and wine ceremony.

It is time to remove the corn and potato from the cauldron, (or take it out of the oven). To eat of this harvest will bring you good luck. Enjoy some of the corn and potato and make a libation of what you don't eat. Before doing a circle closing, hold up your athame, and say:

"*To the gods, merry meet and merry part, and merry meet again. So mote it be.*"

Mabon/Autumn Equinox For a Group

The harvest is in full force. Now is the time to be joyful and celebrate what you are harvesting in your life as well as the earth's bounty.

Decorate your altar with flowers, herbs, nuts and fruit. All should be as colorful as possible. Take an apple, cut it in half and display it by showing the star in the center. Decorate your ritual area with the foliage around the area along with flowers, vegetables and fruits. Have the Wheel of the Seasons on the altar decorated with leaves, flowers and ribbons in the colors of the season. You will need three potatoes cleaned and cut into small pieces. Have fresh rosemary and dill herb with a little butter. You will also need a small container that can go into a fire. Have paper and pens for everyone. Three people will be needed for the blessing.

Begin by erecting your circle in the usual manner. The high priestess rings the bell three times and says:

"*All hail, the harvest is in and plentiful. Let us give thanks for all our blessings.*"

The potato is placed into the container and the herbs and butter are added. The high priestess calls forward the first person for the harvest blessing.

A coven member uses an athame to draw an invoking earth pentagram over the potato, and says:

"*Blessing of the Goddess into this harvest, for it is the fruit of her body which sustains us. All hail Gaia, our great mother.*"

All reply: "*Hail, and blessed be.*"

The second coven member is called forward for the blessing, and says:

"*Blessings of the Goddess Diana, Moon Goddess whose energies we plant our harvest by. All hail Diana.*"

All respond: "*Hail, and blessed be.*"

A third coven member is called to the blessing, and says:

"*Blessings of the great Horned God Herne, whose seeds and energies help bring forth the harvest we all enjoy and celebrate. All hail Herne.*"

All respond: "*Hail, and blessed be.*"

High priestess says:

"*This is also the time we remove the weeds from our gardens so our harvest can come into its fullness. And in our lives we do the same, for we are the same and as one with the earth.*"

The high priest hands out the paper and pens to everyone, and says:

"Take but a moment and decide what are the weeds in your life? What must you remove in order to grow? Write them on the piece of parchment. Then, while holding it in your hand, dance slowly around the cauldron three times, then cast it into the fire while you chant,

"Burn, burn, my heart is free,
Out of my life be gone from me."

As you throw it into the fire, say: "*So mote it be.*"

When all are finished, the high priestess takes up the wand, and says:

"This is the time of the turning of the wheel, the turning of the seasons."

The high priest takes the wheel off the altar and faces the high priestess. They turn the wheel three times, and the high priestess turns to the person on her right and does the same. All in turn do the same. The potatoes are removed from the fire and each person is given a portion to consume. The high priestess says:

"Blessed be, the harvest from our Mother Goddess, that we now part take in her honor. Let it give us life, love, strength and happiness. Blessed be."

Major Sabbat

Samhain, Halloween - October 31st

In Patricia Crowther's book, *Lid off the Cauldron*, the actual date of Samhain is 15 degrees Scorpio. This usually happens between November 8 and 15. The date usually changes each year. Most celebrate it on October 31. The groups I work with celebrate it the weekend nearest to the actual date. This is by far my favorite holiday. The Celts believed that summer turned into winter at this holiday. It is the Witches New Year. Being a Scorpio, working with the underworld fits me very well.

This is the time the vials are thinnest between the spirit world and the physical world. It is the time to reconnect with family members who have passed on. At the Sabbat I attend, every year we have a "Dumb Supper." At the grand table is the place of honor for the spirits that have passed on that year or those you wish to remember. Everyone brings pictures and other items relating to relatives and friends who have died and place them on the sacrificial chair. The chair is always made of wood so it can be burned in honor of the dead. There is a place-setting of our best food and drink. And at the appropriate time there is a procession to the fire and ceremonial burning. It is always a very moving night.

This is also the time for scrying to get a glimpse into the new year. This feast is one of the largest sabbats of the year. Everyone makes his or her favorite foods. The appropriate candles are orange and black. We decorate the circle and the altar with pumpkins, cornhusks, apples and nuts. Preparing for this feast can be great fun. Each year we choose a different theme. One year we did an elemental theme. There were costumes of salamanders, gnomes, undines (mermaids), and faeries. It was an incredible sight to see. So be creative and have fun with this Sabbat.

Samhain Ritual For a Solitary

Carve a pumpkin for your altar. Decorate your Wheel of the Seasons with orange and black ribbons. This is the last harvest, so have all the various vegetables that are plentiful for your altar and circle. You need to place a black mirror and two white candles on the altar. Be sure you have a journal to write in. If you are wearing a robe, it should be black. Have a black shawl to cover your head for the ritual. If you don't have a black shawl, then your robe should be hooded. Since this is the time the great Horned God comes into power, have a statue of him, or horns or antlers on the left side of the altar. Have a cauldron with firewood ready for lighting, or if indoors, place a candle in the cauldron.

Begin your ritual by ringing the bell three times, stop for a moment and ring it three times again, stop for a moment and then ring the bell three more times, making it nine rings in all. Light your altar candles, and say:

"*As the night leads into day,*
So the summer becomes the winter,
And the green turns into gray,
It is he who would guide us,
The children who know the way."

Take the bell and ring it again three times three, as before. Sitting in front of your altar, close your eyes and breathe deeply. Relax your body and mind. Take at least ten deep breaths, feeling your body relaxing and letting go.

Visualize yourself in front of a cave that is deep in a forest. It is dark with only the moon to light your path, but it lights the cave enough for you to see your way. As you walk deeper you notice there is phosphorous on the walls that light the cave as you walk. You begin to smell frankincense burning as you walk deeper into the cave. There is a dark figure sitting in a cutout in the wall. A hand beckons you to come closer. You don't feel any danger, so you approach and sit in front of the hooded figure. You cannot see the person's face, only their hands. A voice speaks to you: "What do you wish to know?" You think for a moment, and then you asked your question. It should be something you have needed an answer to but didn't know who to ask. There is silence for a moment, and once again the voice speaks, giving you an answer. The figure becomes translucent and then disappears.

You continue your journey, contemplating the answer you were given until you come out the other side. There is a lake with a boat waiting for you, and in it a tall, dark, hooded figure. The figure holds out its hand as if asking you for a fee. Three silver coins appear in your palm; you give them to him. You step into the boat and are taken to an island. You can hear dogs barking, but you can't see them. As you step onto the island you can hear someone approaching, so you stand perfectly still. It is the great Horned God.

He speaks to you: "You may come no further into my land, for to do so will keep you here for all time as you know it. Here by the Ancient Crone is the cauldron of knowledge. Come and glimpse the future." You kneel by the foot of the Ancient Crone and look into the cauldron. The smoke and steam begin to form a picture. Keep that image in your mind. The Horned God calls for you to leave with the boatman. You ponder the picture you saw in the cauldron as you are returned to the mainland. You turn to thank the boatman, but he has disappeared. Tired, you sit and lean against a tree. Close your eyes, take a deep breath. When you are ready, you can open them. You find yourself sitting in front of your altar.

Stand now and place the black shawl over your head or pull the hood onto your head. Light the two white candles that are on either side of the black mirror. Focus your attention on the center of the mirror and stare. You will begin to see forms or pictures. Write down what you see.

It is time to light your cauldron and put on some lively dance music. Dance around the circle, calling out your ancestors' names. With each turn, jump over the cauldron. Be sure to make at least three turns. After the cauldron dance it is time to do the cakes and wine ceremony, making a toast to the Horned God and then to your ancestors. Close your circle and begin your feast.

Samhain Ritual For a Group

For this ritual, all should wear their black robes, or if in a public park, black clothing. There should be a black shawl to put over the crone during ritual, or her robe should be hooded. Everyone should bring a carved pumpkin that will line the circle, facing out. A small one should be on the altar with apples, pomegranates and nuts. It is appropriate for the altar candles to be orange and black. They should be anointed with underworld oil. The high priestess should play the part of the Dark Goddess. The high priest should wear his horned helmet and take the place of the Horned God. You need another person to be the challenger who guards the underworld, and a women to play the Ancient Crone sitting by the cauldron. The circle is opened in the usual manner. The high priest stands in the north with his arms crossed in front of his chest holding his sword. The high priestess rings the bell three times three. She now takes the wand and points it in the direction of the high priest, and says:

"*By the flame that burns so bright,*
By sunny day and moonlit night,
In tree groves by forest deep,
Through hidden trails and twisted tree,
We of the craft are drawn to thee,
Here and now at the witching hour,
We call thee forth to lend your power,
Herne, Herne, Herne.
So mote it be."

The high priest then holds his arms and sword out and gives a message to all. This should come naturally from the high priest, speaking for the Horned God. Someone should record the message for future reference. All in the coven should then pass by him and bow or make a sign of honor to him. He thus begins his reign. The guardian and crone take their places at the northeastern point of the circle. The crone sits and is draped with the black shawl. At her feet is a black cauldron filled with water. The guardian stands before her with a sword guarding the crone. One by one, walk and try to pass the guardian. The guardian stops them with his sword, and says:

"*Stop and take heed, traveller,*
Do you have the courage to glimpse the future from the crone's cauldron?"

Each reply: "*I do.*"

Guardian then says: "*Where does the truth appear?*"

Each replies: "*Deep within the Cauldron of the Crone, So Mote It Be.*"

With these words he allows each person to pass. When they pass they kneel at the cauldron and the crone and scry into the cauldron in hopes for a glimpse of how the new year will be. When all have taken their turns, the high priestess and the high priest change places with the challenger and the crone so they too can receive their message. The high priestess then takes up her goblet, and says:

"*Again comes a new year,*
Another chance for new beginnings.
Place the cauldron and light the fire,
Let the dance of life begin."

The cauldron is set in place in front of the altar. The fire is lighted and music or drumming begins. All dance around the circle and jump over the cauldron, calling out their family and ancestors' names. When the dance is done, the ceremony of cakes and wine is shared. The circle is closed and the feast begins.

Minor Sabbat

Yule, December 22nd

Midwinter solstice is the longest night of the year. It is also the turning point when the days begin getting longer and the sun grows in strength. We celebrate the return of the Sun God and warmth to the earth. We decorate our altar and homes with evergreens because they are considered very powerful. They have the strength to withstand winter. Holly, pine and ivy are the favorites to decorate with. We decorate a Yule tree with lights to celebrate the sun's return. Hot cider with cinnamon is served to honor the apple trees for the abundance of fruit they give us. This is a time of great celebration and giving. We in EarthGuard have a tradition at Yule of the burning of the log from the year before. The new log from this year's tree is cut from the bottom of the yule tree and three holes are drilled into it for candles that go on the altar. It is decorated with holly and pine. The candles are red, representing the warmth of the sun returning. This is a time of promise. The log we used last year for the altar is burned. It starts the Yule fire for the present year, once again focusing on the return of the sun.

Wiccan Yule-Tide Gifts

We give gifts at this time, but it's not a matter of going to the store and buying something. Each person constructs a gift that is of a magickal nature. A great deal of thought and energy is put into the making of a Yule gift. Each year we put our names into a bowl, and each person picks a name of a person to make a gift for. I consider this kind of gift a real treasure. I still have some gifts that were made for me 25 years ago.

I once made a wand for a coven member. I went to a park in search of a branch that had fallen on its own. As I walked through the park thinking of the person I chose for a Yule gift,

I came across a perfect-sized branch. It came from a tree that appeared to have been hit by lightning. After I brought it home I cut it to size and removed the bark. I then envisioned the person using the wand in ritual. While doing this I sanded the wand until it had a beautiful, smooth finish. I drilled a hole into the top and glued a quartz crystal point to add to its energy. I decided to blacken the wand by holding it over a candle flame and then rubbing it with a white candle while it was still hot. I then took a cloth and rubbed the excess soot off the wand. This process darkens the wand and gives it a beautiful finish from the wax. The process takes at least an hour. Each time you rub the excess wax off you can see the areas that need more work. By the time you finish working with it you have charged it with the vision you pictured and the love you have for that person. When it is finished, it is a beautiful tool. I then made a velvet bag to keep it in and embroidered symbols of power and protection on it. After the Yule ritual we exchanged our gifts. What a good feeling to see the joy in that person's face when you give them a gift that has a bit of yourself in it. It is so much better than just going to a store and buying a gift. If you don't have someone to exchange with, then make a gift for the Goddess. Choose an area that needs cleaning up and transform it in her honor. There are so many things you can do to create a special Yule gift.

Yule Ritual For a solitary

On your altar with the usual tools have a Yule log with red candles. Decorate it with greenery. Decorate your Wheel of the Seasons with green and red ribbons and twigs of a pine tree. Have a white shawl handy. Build your temple in the usual manner.

Begin your ritual by ringing the altar bell three times, and say:

"Under mountains dark and tall,
In valleys and forests big and small,
Our ancient mother rests,
But is forever understood the life that is within shall soon be manifest."

Sit in front of your altar and breathe deeply. Relax your body and feel yourself floating comfortably. There is a natural light in the distance. It is coming closer and closer. Suddenly, the light reveals a beautiful open valley surrounded by a forest. All is lush and green. You find yourself wanting to lie in the soft green grass. As you do this, in the distance you can see an old woman dressed is black. She has long, white hair. She is our Crone Mother. She stops and looks in your direction and waves her hand over the valley. A soft, white blanket of snow appears. All is covered in white. All is silent. Not even birds or insects can be heard. All are in slumber. You become part of this soft, white snow. You can feel the quiet and the extreme peace it brings with it. But beneath and within you can feel the promise of life. All is as it should be in balance and in peace. A realization comes to you of balance. There is a time of planning and looking within, and a time of doing. This is the time of introspection. This is a time of planning for new things in your life. There is a fine line of balance that needs to be kept in nature. Planning begets doing, so plan well. The crone teaches us that all the answers are within and we need quiet time to discover them. You can feel the silence of the snow that covers you. You don't feel cold. As you sit up, you notice the crone has gone, and coming into the valley is a tall man covered with oak leaves. It is the Oak King . He is walking to the cauldron the crone has left behind. The fire feels good to him as he sits next to it. Deep within the forest comes another man covered with holly leaves. It is the Holly King. He holds up his staff and challenges the Oak King, for only one king at a time can rule. They battle until the Holly King is knocked down, surrendering his rule until the season changes again. All is in balance as it should be. You feel yourself drifting off and see a light coming toward you. You can see your circle now, and when you are ready you can open your eyes.

Stand and take the white shawl and cover your altar with it, and say."

"The Goddess on top of mountains,
The Goddess of carven stone,
The crone of silver fountains,
Shall come into her own.
Blessed be."

Remove the shawl to show the new beginning.

Light the Yule candle, and say:

"The trees shall wave on mountains,
The grass beneath the sun,
His life shall flow like fountains,
The Sun God shall surely come.
So mote it be."

Take the Wheel of the Seasons and turn it three times. It is time to light the cauldron. Put some lively dance music on and dance around the circle, jumping over the cauldron at least three times. It is time to do the cakes and wine ceremony. Make a libation to the Sun God in your own words. Close the circle and feast.

Yule Ritual For a Group

The altar and the circle is decorated the same as for the solitary ritual. Have a place on or beneath the altar for yule gifts. A white shawl is needed for ritual. Once more a male is chosen for the Holly King and the Oak King. It is the turning of the seasons once again.

The ritual begins with ringing of the bell three times.

The high priestess says:

"*Under mountains dark and tall,*
In valleys and forests big and small,
Our Ancient Mother rests,
But is forever understood,
The life within shall manifest."

The high priestess kneels in front of the altar as the high priest covers her with the white shawl, and says:

"*Know that as our lady sleeps,*
Deep within her womb life is being created,
Once more all shall be fruitful,
The balance is maintained,
In her slumber the earth grows strong,
Seek within thyself the same balance,
For all is connected and moves in harmony.
So mote it be."

He removes the shawl and helps her to her feet. The cauldron is put in its place and lighted by the Oak King. He sits besides it. The Holly King starts his joyful dance around the circle with his staff. As he approaches the cauldron to jump over it, the Oak King stops him. He challenges the Holly King with his staff. In battle, the Oak King knocks the Holly King to the ground. The Oak King cries out:

"*The wheel has turned,*
My time is once more,
As of olden times of yore.
Follow me and dance merrily,
All life's renewed as it should be."

Lively music is played and the Oak King leads the cauldron dance. All dance until the fire goes out. The ceremony of cakes and wine is performed, and the high priestess takes the Wheel of the Seasons and begins the turning-of-the-wheel ceremony. When all have had a turn, the wheel is replaced on the altar and the gifts are exchanged. The closing of the circle follows, and then all enjoy the feast.

Chapter 7

Additional Rituals

Finding My Way

By Eileen Smith

Sometimes the road isn't clear to the eye, but the spirit will always connect.
Sometimes the Goddess hides her path, but the senses will always detect
Sometimes your life takes turns that your sense could not expect,
Yet, it brings you to the space you needed so you could grow and project

I wonder soemthimes what could it all mean
Am I headed in the right direction?
Then on a full moon nigh, by candlelight,
Goddess answers all of my questions

As years have passed, and truth be told
Time has proven the ways of old
Here I stand, heart in hand trusting in her ways
Never has she disappointed me,
Not now or till the end of days
So mote it be.

Goddess Ritual of Connection

Have on the altar a white taper candle anointed with Maiden Goddess Oil. Next to it have a red candle anointed with Mother Goddess Oil. Next to the red have a dark-blue candle anointed with Crone Mother Oil. This ritual is meant to open a connection to all three phases of the Goddess within each person. If there are several women in the group, the high priestess may choose three women to play the parts of these phases of the Goddess. The maiden should wear a wreath of flowers in her hair. The mother should wear the crescent moon crown, and the crone should wear a dark shawl.

The high priestess takes Maiden Goddess Oil and anoints the forehead of each person with an invoking earth pentagram. She or the woman playing the maiden lights the white candle, and says:

"*In the light of the first quarter of the moon the Maiden Goddess begins her journey. She who is the beginning, the innocent beauty of the young maiden, the first flow of energy, the beauty of youth, remember her energy deep within you.*"

The high priestess takes Mother Goddess Oil and anoints each person on the palms of their hands with an invoking earth pentagram. She or the woman playing the Mother Goddess lights the red candle, and says:

"*In the light of the full moon the Mother Goddess shines in full sight of all. She illuminates our being. She is the bountiful and fruitful mother which all life springs forth from. She is the loving mother who is the full force of nature's energy flow. Remember her energy deep within you.*"

The high priestess takes Crone Goddess Oil and anoints the back of each person's hands with the invoking earth pentagram. She or the woman playing the crone then lights the dark-blue candle, saying:

"In the dark of the new moon the Ancient Crone holds the secrets of the universe. She gives the understanding of the knowledge learned. Remember her energy deep within you."

The high priestess takes the basket of small white candles around the circle, giving one to each person. When she is back where she began, she lights the first person's candle, saying:

"Let the light of this candle represents the light of the Goddess within you."

Each person then lights the candle of the next person, going deasil, saying the same words until all are lighted. The high priestess holds out her arms, and says:

"All in nature are connected one to each other. All have impact on the earth, and all that exist are one. Feel the youth of the maiden within you, feel the love of the mother about you and the understanding of the crone that comforts you. So mote it be."

Everyone blows out their candles. Dance music is played and all hold hands and dance, raising energy with the chant:

"Maiden, mother and the crone, forever by us, never alone."

After the energy is raised, all drop to the floor and place their palms to the ground sending the energy to the earth. The cakes and wine ceremony is then performed and the circle is closed.

Ritual to Honor the Horned God

In the craft we honor the Goddess. She is the mother of all things living. She is the creator, the giver of life. Also the Horned God, the consort of the Goddess who is the protector and guardian of souls. We know that in nature it takes a male and female together to create. And in the world of the gods, we have always wondered who came first, the God or the Goddess? That is a question that can't be answered. Some things are better left alone. But in their mysteries one thing is certain, and that is the love for us that emanates from them. And so we honor both. This ritual is best done from the autumn equinox to the spring equinox. A circle is erected in the usual manner.

Statue of the Horned God in Lady Diana's outdoor circle

The high priest stands at the north side of the altar with his back to the north. The high priestess stands facing him to the south of the altar, holding a wand. The high priest puts on the horned helmet. The high priestess hands him the sword, and he crosses his arms in front of his chest. The high priestess, using the wand, invokes the Horned God into the high priest, saying:

"Hail, oh ancient god of forest deep,
Lord of the underworld whose souls you keep,
Ye who teaches of things wild and free,
Who gives us comfort, hear our plea,
Come, oh come unto this place,
Whose restless heart we do embrace,
Oh ancient father whose love we feel,
Speak through our priest ___________ here
To bestow on us thy knowledge concealed."

The high priestess draws an invoking pentagram in front of the high priest and chants with a strong voice:

"Ah-EE-Ah-EE-O
Ah- EE-Ah-EE-O
Ah-EE-Ah-EE-O"
Herne, Herne, Herne."

The high priest then speaks the charge of the Horned God.

Charge of the Horned God

"I am the strength and the force that drives all beings to mate and breed, so life continues and can forever succeed.
I am your protector when you pass beyond this land,
I am the lord of the summer land.

Once upon a long time ago, I was worshiped without fear,
Now many turn away when I draw near,
They have forgotten who I am, but I am still here,
For I am lord of kingdoms wild and free, where animals roam and live in harmony.

My lessons clear and forthright can't be misunderstood.
Live in freedom and harmony, take only what you need,
And give back to the mother you worship, but forever take heed.
For I am her consort and I will protect her from harm, always am I with her for our love has created form.

There is another side of me is sure, for know that I am the rumbling during a quake, the mighty winds that make buildings shake.
Let there be no mistake, for I am that power when nature awakes.

Speak my name three times three, like the Goddess I will protect thee.

Remember my words I have passed on to you, that what you've planted in life you will ensue.
So mote it be."

The high priestess bows her head in reverence, and all who pass do the same. The high priest takes off his helmet and gives the high priestess the sword to be returned to the altar. Magick and healing is done at this time. The ceremony of cakes and wine is then performed, followed by the circle closing.

Lady Thelma and Mannan are joined in a handfasting ceremony performed by Lady Diana.

Handfasting, a Joining of Two People

In the ways of the Wiccan, marriage is for a year and a day. If this year is to their liking, they can renew their vows at that time. Some make it a legal and binding ceremony. Many today make it legal and binding at the first ceremony. Handfasting is also for gay couples to celebrate their love for each other. It allows them to bind together in a sacred ceremony.

The circle area is decorated with flowers, grain and fruit. Mead is made from sweet honey for the ceremony. On the altar, in addition to the ritual tools, you will need two small bags, each containing three small stones: hematite for grounding, bloodstone to keep the marriage strong and aventurine for prosperity and healing. Have on hand the marriage oil, a scissor, two pillows made for the couple to kneel on during the ceremony and two nine-foot cords that the couple will wear around their waists. The bride wears a circlet of flowers in her hair, the groom wears a circlet of leaves. A gay couple, if male, would wear greenery with rainbow ribbons interwoven through it. A female gay couple would wear greenery with baby's breath and white ribbons.

It is customary for the bride to wear a silver robe and the groom to wear a gold robe. This represents the Goddess and the God. Or they can choose to wear green with a silver and gold cord around their waists. A gay male couple can wear red with gold cords or lavender robes with white cords. A gay female couple can wear green robes with silver cords or white robes with red cords. All represent the purity of love (white), abundance of love (green), passion of love (red) and the spiritual side of love (lavender). These are suggestions; the couple will select their preferred color scheme.

For the ceremony, someone is designated to sweep in front of the couple. This is usually one or both of the couple's mothers or close friends. The sweeping is a clearing away of any negative vibrations so the couple has a good start in life.

There can be a flower person to sprinkle flower pedals before the couple, a maid or man of honor who attends to the bride and groom before and during the ritual. The maid or man of honor helps them get ready and anoints their hands during the ceremony. The circle is opened in the usual manner with an additional announcement at each corner, such as:

"*Take heed, oh mighty ones, a handfasting is to be witnessed. So mote it be.*"

It is common for a couple to pick music for their entrance. Sometimes different music for each partner's entrance, such as a favorite song they have for each other. When the music starts, the person sweeping clears a path for the couple, sweeping into the sacred space and making one complete turn around the circle. The sweeper then leaves the besom by the altar and takes a place to the left of the high priestess. The flower person follows, throwing flowers and grain before the couple. The couple enters with the maid and man of honor and walks one full turn around the circle, stopping in front of the altar. The maid and man of honor prepares the couple by anointing their hands with the marriage oil. They draw an invoking earth pentagram on their palms and then kisses or hugs them.

The high priest takes the wand and draws an invoking earth pentagram in front of the bride, saying:

"*Oh great mother of all creation, here before you is your image. Within him/her are the powers of love, desire and pleasures beyond all thoughts and creation. She/he is a true reflection of you. I invoke you and call upon you, Gaia and Diana, into this priestess/priest so all that comes from this union will be blessed. So mote it be.*"

The high priestess then takes the wand and draws an invoking earth pentagram in front of the groom, saying:

"Hear ye, oh great Horned God of the green wood, hear my call. Before you stands your reflection. Within him / her is the power to protect, to provide, to give comfort, to love, (for a straight couple) and to give life through his seed. I invoke and call upon you, great Herne of the green wood, to enter this priest / priestess, protect this union so that all that comes from it will be blessed. So mote it be."

For a gay couple, the high priest/high priestess takes the wand and draws an invoking earth pentagram in front of the couple, saying:

"Hear ye, oh great force of the universe. You who are the beginning of all things before form and contain the knowledge of both the God and the Goddess, I invoke you. Grant this couple protection so their union can endure all adversities that might come their way. Let their union be filled with abundance of understanding, kindness and compassion for one another. Let their union be blessed, for all acts of love are sacred to the gods. So mote it be."

The high priestess places the pillows in front of the altar. The couple removes the cords from around their waists and hands them to the high priestess and the high priest. The couple kneels facing each other and holds each other's forearms. The high priest takes the cord and wraps it around the left side of their forearms three times without making a knot, and says:

"Bound are thy arms willingly,
But ever free,
Bound is your love for eternity,
But ever free.
So mote it be."

The high priestess takes the other cord and wraps the right forearms three times without making a knot, and says:

"Bound are thy lives willingly,
But ever free,
Bound by the body and heart,
But ever free.
So mote it be."

The high priestess and high priest cut a small snippet of hair from the bride and groom. The hair is placed in the bags containing the stones. The cords are removed and the bags are given to them. The first partner hands the bag to his or her partner, and says:

"Carry this with you when we are apart, then I will always be with you."

The second partner gives does the same, and says:

"Carry this with you so whenever we are apart, know that a part of me will always be with you."

The first partner makes his or her vow to the second partner and places a ring on the heart finger of his/her left hand. The second partner does the same. The couple kisses and embraces. At this time all the guests that are in the circle hold hands and dance around the couple, chanting:

"Life and love and loyalty,
Growth, abundance and prosperity
are forever theirs. So mote it be."

When the dance is finished, the energy is sent to the couple. The maid and man of honor helps the bride and groom up. They stand in front of the altar holding their cords. The maid and man of honor hold the other end of the cords and express a wish for the couple. Then they tie a knot, putting that energy into the cords. All in turn do the same. Finally, the high priestess and the high priest seal the knots with a double

knot and another wish. The cords are then given to the couple to hang in their home for good luck.
The high priestess then says:

"May your union last as long as your love lasts,
May your love last for all of your life together."

The high priest says (for a straight couple):

"For the first time upon this earth let me introduce to you
the lord and lady of the day, Mr. and Mrs. ____________."

(for a gay couple):

"For the first time upon this earth let me introduce to you this perfect couple, ____________ and ____________."

The high priestess and high priest then perform the ceremony of cakes and wine, beginning by offering the couple the food and drink to celebrate their first meal together.

A circle is then closed. At this time the besom is held for the couple to jump over. All in the circle follow by jumping the broom. The feast and merriment follows.

Home Blessing

A home blessing is good to do when someone moves into a new residence. It clears the energy that was left behind by the old tenants or, in the case of a new home, the workers who built it. It is also good to do if there have been a lot of problems or arguing in a home. It's always good to start with a clean slate. This way the home will contain only the energy those living there put into it.

You will need to set up a simple altar in the center of the house. On it place a dish of water, a dish of salt, a dish of clearing oil, sage, nag champa incense or another sweet incense, flowers, a white candle, forty new pennies and sweet bread or cake. It is good to invite people you love to be part of the home blessing.

Begin by having everyone holding hands in a circle in front of the altar. If you are doing the blessing by yourself, stand in front of the altar with your arms outstretched. Visualize a blue white pentagram above your head. See it growing and growing in height and width until it pushes out every bit of the surrounding vibrations out into the universe. You or the high priestess light the white candle, and say:

"*By friendly spirits whose hearts are loyal,*
By water, salt and sacred oil,
By candle flame and burning herbs,
All is clear and will be preserved."
"*So mote it be.*"

You or the high priestess take the sage and light it, starting at the front door. Then walking widdershins (counterclockwise) through every room in the house, ending at the front door. The front door is opened and the sage is buried in front of the house. If this is an apartment, it can be buried in front of the building. The high priestess then takes the besom and sweeps through the house, starting at the front door and going through all the rooms widdershins, saying:

"*Besom, besom, the Wiccans' broom,*
Doth clear this place of dark and doom.
From ancient times to the present day,
Here and now all is sweep away.
So mote it be."

She (or yourself) returns to the front door. The door is opened and the sweeping ends just outside of the home. The high priestess returns to the altar and consecrates the salt and water in the usual manner. Three pinches of the salt are put into the water and stirred three times. The resident takes the dish of consecrated water and, beginning at the front door, sprinkles it while moving through the rooms clockwise and ending at the front door. The sweet incense is lighted and the homeowner repeats the same walk through the house. The forty pennies are distributed among all who are participating. Lively music is played and all dance throughout the home, throwing pennies into the corners of each room while chanting:

"*Abundance and wealth,*
Good friends and good health."

All return to the altar. You or the high priestess take the sealing oil and draw an invoking earth pentagram above the front door while saying:

"*This doorway is sealed,*
Nno evil may pass,
From this time forward,
Shall forever last."

The high priestess returns to the altar and performs the cakes and wine ceremony. A toast is made by someone chosen to say something front the heart. You or the high priestess holds the ritual cup, and says:

"*May our wishes of love, joy, abundance, good health and a wealth of good friends forever be the heart of this home.*
So mote it be."

All repeat: "*So mote it be.*"

Good-luck gifts are given for the home by all attending, and all join in a feast.

Wiccaning, Blessing and Naming of a Child

This ritual is to acknowledge a child's entrance into the world, to name him/her and to ask for guidance and protection from the gods so their paths will have direction. It is also to give them a Goddess parent to help them on their way. This spiritual bond is for their lifetime.

Have on the altar a dish of earth and a dish of water.

The high priestess says:

"*This child has chosen these parents to learn its lessons on the earth. You (mothers name) and you (fathers name) have given this child a great gift that is the gift of life. May the Goddess give you the patience to listen, to give direction, and may love be the guide in all your decisions.*"

The high priest says:

"*Within the birth of a new spirit lies the future of all his/her ancestors. With his/her accomplishments brings joy and fulfillment to all they who came before him/her. Within your little hands lies the future of the universe.*"

The high priestess says:

"*What name have you given to this child?*"

Parents respond "______________ *is his/her name.*"

The high priestess says:

"*Take now your child to the four directions and proclaim him/her to the guardians.*"

The child is taken first to the eastern quarter and held up by the parents.

The father says:

"Take heed, oh guardians of the east, before you is _______. Give to him/her the protection against any adversity and give to him/her the knowledge to seek his/her true path and to always see the Goddess in all things."

The child is then taken to the south and held up.

Father says:

"Take heed, oh guardians of the south, before you is ___________. Give to him/her the protection against any adversity and give to him/her the power to use his/her will wisely."

The child is taken to the west, and the mother says:

"Take heed, oh guardians of the west, before you is ___________. Give to him/her the protection against any adversity and give him/her the power to understand and to be able to control his/her emotions throughout his/her life."

The child is taken to the north, and the mother says:

"Take heed, oh guardians of the north, before you is ___________. Give to him/her the protection against any adversity and give to him/her the power to know when to be silent."

The child is brought to the front of the altar, and the parents proclaim before the coven:

"Be it known to all that this new person shall be ever known as ___________."

The high priestess says:

"Who here is the Goddess parent for this child?"

Goddess parent steps forward, and says:

"I _________ shall be________ spiritual guide upon the earth. I will love, protect, teach and guide this child from this moment forward."

The goddess parent takes the child into her/his arms and visualizes a silver umbilical cord attached from herself to the child's navel. The goddess parent gives her/his vow to the child and anoints it with Goddess Oil. She/he does this by putting a very small amount of the oil on their fingertips and touching the child's right breast, left breast, navel and right breast.

The goddess parent says:

"I consecrate you and ask for the guidance of Goddesses Gaia and Diana. I consecrate and ask for the protection of the Horned God Herne. May he forever protect you from all harm or adversity."

The goddess parent takes the child to each coven member so each can give a blessing and a spiritual gift to the child. This is done by each member placing their hands on the child and wishing them good health, intelligence, etc. The goddess parent returns to the front of the altar with the child.

The high priestess says:

"As the sun comes up each morning in the starting of a new day, so shall the earth and the universe be affected by this new life. Even as a single grain of sand is moved, it too affects all that is. So shall (child's name) have impact on the earth and all who dwell upon it. May (child's name) *learn about loving all those who are part of his/her life."*

The high priest says:

"May (child's name) *learn compassion for all those who are less fortunate than himself/herself. May he/she learn to listen and take time to nourish his/her own spirit, for humans can get lost in the matters of living."*

The goddess parent cuts a piece of hair from the child and puts it aside to be buried with a tree that will be planted in the name of the child. The goddess parent takes a little bit of earth and puts it on the child's hand, and says:

"This is part of the earth you live on. She nourishes your spirit with her beauty, and she will feed your body. Always respect her and give back to her. Never take more from her than you need."

The goddess parent pours water over the child's hands to rinse off the earth, and says:

"This is the water of the earth that cleans your hand. It will quench your thirst, and the life within it will feed you as well. Always respect it and keep it clean for the generations that will follow you. Never take from it more then you need."

The goddess parent then blows into the child's face, and says:

"This is the air we breathe, it sustains life within us. Always respect it and keep it clean. Always protect your environment;

never be afraid to stand up for it. Protect it for generations to come after you."

The child is then given back to its parents.

The high priest says:

"This is a celebration of life. (Child's name), go forth and live it in honor of the Goddess and your ancestors. So mote it be."

It is time for the ceremony of cakes and wine with a feast to follow.

Wiccan Funeral

In witchcraft we deal with death differently than most. We have our time of mourning, but we also celebrate the deceased person's new life to come. It is all a journey of life, death and rebirth. There is so much to learn in this universe that being reborn into another body and continuing the journey makes sense to us. There is a special gift that comes with the craft. After you die, if you lived within the laws of nature -- "An it harm none, do as you will." -- you will be reborn with the loved ones you loved and will know and love them again. Death is in the cycle of life, and we do not fear it. We know we will be reborn in another body and continue our journey.

For this ritual, you will need two black and two white taper candles on the altar. They should be anointed with frankincense oil. It is helpful to have something on the altar from the person who passed. At each corner is one black candle and one white candle. The black candle represents death and passing, the mourning of the loved one. The white candle represents the new life to come. All in attendance need a black shawl large enough to drape over the head and body over their robes. The Wheel of the Seasons should have white ribbons tied on with white flowers (silk is best), then draped with a small black cloth and leaning up in the center of the altar. The circle is erected in the usual manner.

The high priest or a family member takes an athame and goes to the north, draws an invoking earth pentagram, and says:

"I *invoke and call upon thee, oh great Horned God of the underworld. Accept this our brother/sister into your care. Take them to a place where they can forget this life so they can start anew. Hail and blessed be.*"

Each person goes to the north and says what they need to say to the soul that has departed from this world. After this is completed, all remove their shawls of mourning. The high priest or a family member lights the white candle from the black and extinguishes the black candle from the altar and the four corners.. The high priestess or the family member then takes the wand and goes to the east and draws an invoking earth pentagram, saying:

"I invoke the great mother Gaia, mother of the earth and of all living things. Accept this soul back in your womb so he/she may find their way back to us in perfect love and perfect trust. So mote it be."

The high priestess then takes the Wheel of the Seasons off the altar and removes the black cloth to reveal the white flowers and ribbons. This represents rebirth. The high priestess and the high priest turn the wheel between them three times, representing the rebirth of the soul.

Lively dance music is played. All dance to celebrate the return of their brother/sister to the earth when it is time for their return.

The ceremony of cakes and wine is performed and circle is ended in the usual manner.

Chapter 8

Magickal Workings

Journey with the Goddess

To journey with the gods is a special magical experience, one that will affect the connection you have with the Goddess. If you are not sure who to journey with, it is best to have a good connection with the Goddess that you work within ritual. I would suggest beginning with Goddess Diana. All journeys take three months to complete. You start by researching the myths of Diana. You will find she has counterparts in other pantheons. It is important you read and learn all that is connected with her. Here are steps you will need to complete before you actually journey with her.

1. Research and know all aspects connected with the Goddess.

2. Make note of her season and times of year she was honored.

3. Make note of the colors, flowers, incense, tools and symbols associated with her.

4. Collect these things as you go along. If you can't find something you feel is important. then make a miniature of the symbol or have a picture of it.

5. Once you have read and collected what you need, you must write a ritual to honor her.

6. Schedule a full moon night that you will be able to perform the ritual, bringing her into your life.

For the night of your ritual, in addition to your usual altar setup, you will need all the things that you collected for her. You will need to make an altar cloth for her and place all these things on it. This cloth will also serve to wrap everything in order to store it away for the farewell ritual.

Within your ritual you need to add a "calling." This is an invocation you write from your heart and a visualization you will use to bring her into yourself. After you perform the ritual, sit in front of your altar and breathe deeply. You must relax your body completely. When you have done this, visualize the Goddess in the surroundings you would expect her to be in from your research. See yourself within a circle before her. See her coming toward you and coming into your circle. At that moment, see yourself opening your arms to her. As she approaches, she turns around directly in front of you. The Goddess will then become translucent and step back into you. Feel her inside of you. Feel the incredible love the Goddess has for you. Thank her for coming to journey with you. From this day and for thirty days, all that you experience will be with her influence.

Gather all the things you collected for this ritual and wrap them in the altar cloth you made for her. You must put them away for thirty days. At the end of thirty days you must have another circle for her with all her things. But this time instead of a calling you must thank her from your heart and say farewell. Once again, sit in front of your altar and relax your body. Again, visualize yourself at the same place and within your circle. Now visualize a blue-white pentagram on your back. Feel it pushing through you helping the Goddess out of your body. Now see her standing in front of you. She smiles at you and embraces you. You thank her for all you have learned on your journey. See her leave your circle and walk off into her own world. Then bring yourself back. Collect everything you had for her and place it in a special box. End your circle in the usual manner. Now take thirty days to write about your journey. Each day write something you remember that you felt regarding the Goddess being part of. She has left a little of herself with you. You now have a special connection with her. If you need help, she will be there for you.

Give yourself time and then start a journey with Gaia or Herne. You will be amazed with your spiritual growth as you do these journeys. In the future you can journey with other gods and goddesses in whatever pantheon you wish to explore. There are many pantheons you can work with. You can also journey with different things in nature, such as trees and flowers. It is the spirit of them you journey with, and everything has something to teach you. You are the only person that can limit your possibilities.

Writing Chants to Raise Power

Inspired by Lady Khrinn

A simple chant said over and over can raise power within. It can also put you in an altered state. Writing chants is not difficult. All you need to do is focus on the work that needs to be done. This is the place to begin. For example:

I remember a Samhain in 1991 when Patricia Crowther came for a visit from England. Witches came from all over the United States to meet her. We thought it would be a good time to do magick as there would be so many people to raise the energy. Patricia is a staunch advocate for animal rights. She brought with her articles about monkeys that were being used for experiments in England. There was a company called Shamrock Farms that was importing monkeys for that purpose. The torture was horrible and the cruelty was beyond belief. We wanted to raise power to stop these atrocities.

Before our traditional Samhain ritual we enacted a ritual we composed for the animals of the earth. The ritual had several parts to it. There where people who dressed and took the parts of different species of animals. Patricia played the Goddess. Each animal stepped forward to plead his or her case to the Goddess, and Patricia blessed each one. We had composed a chant earlier to direct the energy that went something like this: "Break the chain to Shamrock Farms, so that the monkeys come to no harm." Three circles were formed to dance and raise energy with this chant. Patricia and I directed the energy as everyone danced, and it was very powerful. Three weeks later we received a newspaper clipping from Patricia that told about how Shamrock Farms was closed down because of mistreatment of monkeys. What a good feeling it was to receive the news.

Magick works when it flows smoothly and the vision is clear. Remember, always keep it simple.

There were several of us who got together to compose the chant for the magickal working. The first question we asked ourselves was where was the focus? We wanted to stop Shamrock Farms from importing monkeys, and we wanted the monkeys to be free from harm. We started with a list:

1. Stop Shamrock Farms.
2. Stop the cruelty.
3. Keep the monkeys safe.

The first part of the chant we all agreed upon was "Stop the cruelty of Shamrock Farms." The word we needed to rhyme with was farms. The next thought was, stop the cruelty to what? The monkeys, but it had to rhyme with farms. So we asked ourselves, what did we want for the monkeys that would rhyme with farms? We wanted the monkeys to be free from harm. Harm, this was the word for the rhyme. So it had to end with harm in order for it to rhyme. We also wanted the monkeys to be free. Here was the key. So we kept on saying it in different ways until it flowed. "Stop the cruelty of

Shamrock Farms, free the monkeys from all harm." When we could say the statement easily and our minds caught it with ease, we knew we had our chant. We had about 150 people we needed to teach the chant to right before they were going to use it. So it had to be short and easy to put to memory. The amazing thing about chants is they stick in your memory without having to work hard at memorizing them.

Just remember the best chants are short, easy to remember and rhyme. Start with the main theme. For us, it was shutting down Shamrock Farms. The second part was to protect the monkeys. If rhyming doesn't come easy to you, then buy a rhyming book. There are several on the market and they help when you reach a block. Once you start writing chants, be sure to put them in your Book of Shadows. You never know when they will come in handy for something. Just by changing a word here and there you have a new chant to work with. Chanting is a powerful tool.

Creating Your Own Ritual

Inspired by Illa

Writing your own ritual can be empowering. It might seem difficult at first, but it isn't. I've seen people who have said to me, "I can't write, it's impossible," write some of the most beautiful rituals. Ritual is a way of expressing your spirituality. Rituals are a way of expressing yourself in many different ways. When I get up each morning, I first go to the bathroom, then I drink two cups of coffee. Next I take a shower, get dressed and eat breakfast. Then I brush my teeth and do my makeup. This is my personal ritual. In life there are many rituals such as Wiccaning a child, getting married, graduating from school, etc. Rituals can be filled with joy or sad, such as a funeral.

In Wicca we have rituals for the phases of the moon, honoring the Goddess and God, and celebrating the seasons. Sometimes we need a ritual for a special occasion. Where do we start?

1. Start with a theme such as bringing love into your life.

2. Decide the date you are doing this ritual.

3. Look up the astrological aspects for that day. Be sure they complement the work

4. Which Goddess is known for love?

5. What is associated with this Goddess?

6. Write down a list of things you need to collect.

7. You want to have appropriate incense, oil, flowers and symbols associated with that Goddess.

8.What kind of love are you looking for?

9.What will your image be? You want to see that image in your mind during your ritual.

10.You need an offering, such as sweet wine and cakes.

Suppose you were working with Goddess Aphrodite, one of the best known goddesses of love and beauty. One of the symbols you would need for her altar is the scallop shell. You could also have a statue or picture of a dolphin and a dove. These are sacred symbols associated with her. Red roses would be the flower of choice because they are given to show love. Have a honey wine for an offering and some sweet cakes as well. All add to the experience. With this information begin to write your ritual.

What is the purpose of the love ritual? If you were doing this with a group you would need to have a discussion about the purpose so all are of a like mind. All would need to write down three phases that come into their mind pertaining to the goal.

Now read your phases out loud and compare. See where the thought patters are forming.

1. True love
2. Compassionate love
3. Long-lasting love
4. Perfect person for you

What are some of the aspects of a ritual? You need to engage the senses as much as possible, altering consciousness. Here is where the change occurs. What should the ritual be composed of?

1. Clear vision.
2. A calling to the Goddess for assistance.
3. A chant to raise the power for the work.
4. A declaration of the work to be done.
5. An offering for the completion of work done.

These are the steps to begin with. I would start with writing a calling to the Goddess of love.

The Calling:

"Hail Aphrodite, goddess of love and beauty,
Lend thy powers to this work so my love can find me,
Let it be a magnet for my love to be. So mote it be."

Next I would write a declaration of purpose, such as:

The Purpose

"Beautiful Goddess, guardian of love,
Weave thy powers, your aid thereof,
In this world my love must be,
Help our paths to cross. So mote it be."

Make an oil and incense for the rite. Some of the oils appropriate would be: rose, orrisroot, patchouli, musk, orange, jasmine, lavender and gardenia. Blend together what is pleasing to you. Start with the rose oil and add a few drops of the other oils until you achieve the scent you are looking for. You don't need to use all of these. Keep a record of the formula for later use.

To make the incense, you can use some of the following: rose petals, chamomile flowers, coriander, dried orange peel, sandalwood, cedar wood and cinnamon. You can add to it some of the love oil you have prepared. Follow the instructions in "The Making of Incense" chapter.

It is time to put it all together. You want to place a sea blue-green altar cloth on your altar. If that color is not available, a pink or red cloth will do. Place on your altar, along with the usual tools, the shell or shells, the flowers, incense and oil you prepared for the rite. The candles should be red and anointed with the love oil.

Begin your rite after you erect your temple in the usual manner. Take your bell and ring it three times to bring attention to the rite. Say the calling and burn some of the incense. Next ring the bell three times and state the purpose. Then anoint yourself with the oil - or if a group is involved, the high priestess anoints each person with an invoking earth pentagram near the heart and on the forehead. At this point put on some lively dance music and dance to raise energies, saying the chant you composed. You will be visualizing a person coming in your direction. Do not put a face to this person. Let the Goddess choose for you as she knows best. After the energy is sent out with that visualization it is time to make an offering to the Goddess in the form of a cakes and wine ceremony as a thank-you for the help she gave you. When all is complete, the circle is closed. Then you must make yourself available to meet your soul mate.

Take it one step at a time and be as creative as you like. If you are writing a ritual for a group, you can give each person a small part. It is like writing a mini play. When you put it all together it feels wonderful. You can write rituals for all occasions or for a particular purpose. You will see after you write your first ritual that it will come easy. Keep a record of your rituals by putting them in your Book of Shadows. The Book of Shadows is a growing record of your magickal work.

A Wiccan's Magickal Way of Losing Weight

Losing weight can be a difficult thing to do. Diets can be difficult to maintain. There is a magickal way to help keep you on track. There is a spell for losing weight that works well. To start, you will need a bar of soap. If you have time you can make your own soap for this purpose. There is a section in this book on making magickal soap for different purposes. But if you are like many of us and have little spare time, any soap will work just fine. You will also need a fertilized egg or a drop of your own blood. You can find the eggs at a health food store. They are considered a living organism. Most people are squeamish about pricking their own finger, so they use the fertilized egg to represent a living form. Next you will need a picture of yourself that you would like to look like again. If you don't have one, cut a picture out of a magazine of someone whose figure you would like to have. Place a picture of your own face on it. Finally, you will need a red bag for the soap. There are symbols you will need to draw or embroider on the bag with a marker, such as ogham symbols. The ogham is an ancient Irish tree alphabet. The symbols contain certain energies that can help your magickal journey for losing weight.

The Beith: Birch for a new start, and cleansing.

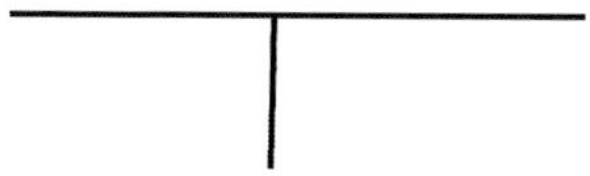

The Duir: Oak for protection and strength

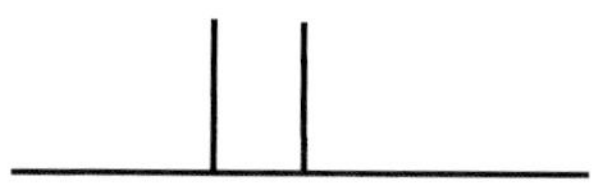

The Ur: Heather for inner self and all healing

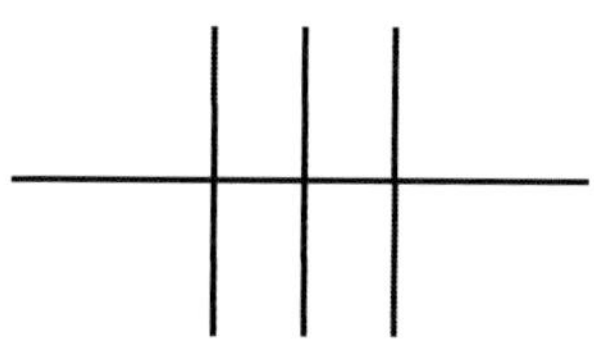

It's best to follow a diet you know that will work for you. All diets work if you stick to them. But this time you will do it magickly. Write a chant, or you may use the one I use for this purpose. It's important to memorize it. Chant this three times before you eat a meal.

Chant For Losing Weight

"Power within, my strength set in,
All work well done, with strength I've won.
So mote it be."

Begin your journey by making a reasonable goal for the week. Since the first week you most likely will be losing water weight, five pounds is a reasonable goal. Only weigh yourself once a week. Try to weigh on the same scale and at the same time. When you see some weight loss, take your athame and shave some of the soap away while chanting the spell. Keep a journal of your weekly weigh in. Be sure you take notice of how the phases of the moon affect your weight loss. Keep tract of each quarter phase as well as the new moon and the full moon. Write it next to the date each week. You will be able to see if there is a pattern to how you lose weight. Do not plan further than a week. It is easier to reach small goals than long-term goals. Remember if you feel you are about to break your diet, chant the spell three times to give you strength. It works if you stick to it.

The Magickal Money Box to Increase Prosperity

This is for those who seem to always have problems with money -- obtaining it or keeping it. This magickal strategy works one hundred percent, but you must follow it to the letter. Money is only a tool we use in our lives to create a better life materially. Too many people just wish for it, while others think someday it will come to them. You have come to the earth to learn physical lessons, as well as spiritual and emotional lessons. If you have to worry about your daily bread, when will you have time to be spiritual? All must be in a state of balance to maintain happiness. The Money Box is a special and unique way to overcome money problems. You must have patience and be steadfast. If you should falter, just begin all over again. If you falter three times, you are not ready for this.

You will need a box. It should be a little larger then a dollar bill and at least three inches high. Paint your box forest green, inside and out. With gold paint, draw prosperity symbols on the inside of the bottom of the box. These are symbols you personally feel will aid your quest for prosperity. On the inside of the lid, paint the earth rune symbol for money and prosperity:

On the top of the cover, paint an earth invoking pentagram. On the bottom of the box, paint a silver triple moon and beneath it a gold Horned God symbol.

Triple Goddess

Horned God

You are ready to begin the journey to prosperity.

Step 1. Take 10 percent of your earnings after taxes and place it into the box. This might be difficult at first, but it is worth doing. Do not put change in the box, only bills. If your 10 percent comes out to be a number such as $35.42, then put $36 in the box. Always round the amount off to the next highest number. Ten percent is important because it is the universal number for money. So never put in less, or it will not work. You may put in more if you like. Put all other money that comes to you, such as a bonus or a gift, into the box.

Step 2. Your box is yours alone and may not be seen or touched by anyone. Keep your box in a secret place. This is a magickal working and should only contain your vibration.

Step 3. The second time you put money in the box, and every time after, you must recount the money. That is, first place the money into the box, then take all of it out and count it. The amount will always increase, because you only count the money after putting 10 percent into it.

Once again, never count the money unless you put money into the box first. This will begin to change how you think about money. Money is only a tool to success. Success is within you.

I have witnessed many wondrous things happen to people who have done this. Some began to find money, and others have told me money was returned to them that they never expected to get back. They began to become a money magnet. But with all good things there are rules you must follow.

Step 4. You must do this for no less then six months. You may never take out a single dollar from the box until six months has passed. After six months, put the last 10 percent in the box, then take all the money out and recount it. Then take 10 percent of that amount and place it back into the box. Put the box away.

Step 5. You now have a nice sum of money, but you must not spend it. That's right, you can't spend it. You must invest it in something that will make you more money. You can put a down payment on a house or buy some works of art. They will increase in value. But you cannot buy a car, because it will depreciate -- unless you use the car for work, which helps you make money. You can put it into mutual funds or other traditional investments if you like. Just remember that this money must make money. You may spend the money it makes, but never the principal.

Now, begin the process again. You already have ten percent in the box from the first time. Use that as another starting point. If you do this a second time and succeed, you will never be without again. That one year's principal will give you a security with money you lacked in the past. Then watch what happens. You will begin to become a money magnet. Money will come to you in different ways. I have had people tell me they found money in the street after they started this. Nothing ever happened like this to them before. Other received rebates they didn't know were coming. It's amazing how it works, so stick to it.

The Art of Making Incense

In order to create the proper atmosphere in your circle you will need to burn incense. You can buy incense easily enough today. But there are times you need something special. It's always better to create your own incense. There are many books you can buy with all kinds of recipes. They're fun to work with, but the way I find most useful is by experimenting. You learn so much more that way. Your senses are as individual as your fingerprints. You need to experiment with herbs, spices, flowers, barks, woods, oils and resins. These are the ingredients needed to make good incense. You can start from your own kitchen and back yard. Know what you are working with. Some things in nature can be dangerous to burn. Take your time and be patient. You need to determine for yourself what each scent evokes in you and what energy is most suited to your purpose. Keep in mind your goals, approach and other contributing factors.

Some of the tools you will find useful are: mortar and pestle, coffee grinder, eyedroppers, measuring spoons, measuring cups, glass or ceramic bowls, and pen and paper.

The pen and paper is extremely important for keeping a record of your recipes. I can remember when I first started making my own incense. One year for Yule I made incense for a gift. I tried to take into consideration the person, their astrological sign and personality. I was really enjoying customizing incense for a special gift. As I worked on it, I kept adding this and that, and more of this and that. I became weary of writing down what I was adding to the formula. Well, the incense was a big hit. But when I was asked for the recipe, I couldn't reproduce it. Of course, as I recall that incense, it was the best I ever made.

Make a list of the herbs you will be working with. You need to test each herb according to its scent and the feeling it brings up in you. Light a charcoal and place it in a small cauldron or receptacle. Let it form a light ash before you place the herbs on it. Now take a small amount of an herb and place it on the hot charcoal. As you smell it, ask yourself these questions: What feeling does it give me? What does it remind me of? Record those answers for the herb. Test only three in a row, then clear your head by going outside for a couple of minutes, or sniff a little ammonia. I suggest the former. If you try to continue without a break, everything will begin to smell the same. Continue to test all the herbs, woods, flowers, resins and oils. This is something you want to add to your Book of Shadows. It will be useful throughout your studies.

Making Incense

When you are ready to make your incense, have on hand glass bowls, measuring tools, grinder, mortar and pestle, and pen and paper. Be sure to store what you make in a tightly covered glass jar away from light, and in a cool dry place. After choosing your ingredients, start by grinding the herbs and flowers (dry ingredients) together in your coffee grinder. This will give the mix a fine texture. Remember that once you use the coffee grinder for making incense you will never be able to use it for grinding coffee again. So keep a special grinder just for incense. Burn some of this mixture on charcoal and smell it. Can you begin to get the feeling you are looking for? You will notice it will burn up quickly. This is why you need to add resins and oils, so your incense will burn for a while. If you are adding powdered wood or bark, add it to the dry ingredients. Stir while giving it your vision. It is just as important as the ingredients you chose. In most cases you can purchase the barks and woods in a powdered form. Burn a little of this mixture, and smell it. Be sure you make notations of the formula as you go along.

Next, grind the resin with your mortar and pestle, visualizing the purpose of the incense. You can never grind the resins in the coffee grinder or it will clog the cutter. Resin should be one part to three parts of dry ingredients. Mix all very well and burn a little to see if you are getting the results you want.
The last ingredients you mix in are the oils. The incense should be moist but not wet. If for some reason you are not happy with what you made, don't throw it out. There is never a batch too bad that some fragrant oils or resin can't fix. Herbs can be expensive, so never throw anything out. Sometimes the ingredients need time to blend together. It is good to place what you made on a plate and put it where the sun can charge it. Then put it where the moon rays can add energy as well. This will take a few days. A quick way to blend the incense is by placing the mixture on a plate and heating it in a microwave oven on defrost for a couple of minutes. When

you see it starting to blend together, stop the microwave. Try a little to see how it is. If you achieved the desired formula, then you can put it in the sun's and moon's rays for charging. Believe me, you will impress yourself as your creation comes together.
When writing your recipe, use the measurements in parts. This way you can easily make large or small amounts just by using the parts system. One part can be a teaspoon or a cup.

Here is a list of herbs that you should have in your magickal pantry. They can easily be found at the grocers, a health food store or a metaphysical bookstore. Some you may even find in your back yard.

When you begin, be sure to compare what you feel about each ingredient to what it is commonly used for. The results are always interesting.

Herb	**Flowers**	**Resin**	**Roots**	**Wood**	**oil**	**Has been known to be used for**
Alfalfa						Increase resources, money
Almond						Consecration, love, communicating with the gods
Aloe						Healing, protection, love, beauty
Anise seed						fertility, consecration, love, protection
Anise					X	Consecration, protection, banishing
Apple bark						Fertility, visions
Arrow root						Good fortune
				Ash		Love, fertility, protection
Basil						Purification, protection, initiation
Bay Laurel					X	Love, visions, funerals
				Beech		Protection, fairy realm-midsummer
Birch						Driving away negative, protection

Blackberry leaves		Health, healing
Camphor		Purification , vision
Caraway		Consecration, love , protection
Catnip		Fertility, visions, cat magick
Cedar	X	Consecration, summer, money
Celery Seed		Divination
Chamomile		Success, love, clearing
Cinnamon	X	Consecration, purification, protection
Clove	X	Increases psychic, attraction
Comfrey		Healing, safe travel, protection
Coriander		Protection, love, immortality
Cumin	X	Attraction, love, protection
Cypress		Funeral, reincarnation
Daisies		Protection, happiness
Dandelion		Love, making wishes come true
Dill		Protection, good luck
Dogwood		Protection, guards Book of Shadows
Elder		Healing, protection
Endive	X	Open doorways of knowledge
Eucalyptus		Purification
Fennel		Strength against danger, midsummer
Fern		Vision, invisibility, midsummer
Fir needles	X	Wisdom
Frankincense	X	Consecration, purification, protection
Ginger		Good health, consecration
Heather	X	Initiation, passion, Lammus
Holly		Protection, funerals
Honeysuckle	X	Visions
Hyssop		Consecration, purification
Jasmine	X	Dress candles, good health

Kava Kava	X	Visions, love
Lavender	X	Consecration, love, vision
Lemon		Love
Lilac		Diva work, love
Lilly-of-the-Valley	X	Fairy work, powerful magick
Lotus	X	Protection, consecration
Marigold		Love, consecration, visions
Marjoram		Love, beauty
Myrrh	X	Ritual, consecration
Narcissus	X	Ritual
Oak		Fertility, strength, protection
Orange	X	Love, fertility
Parsley		Success, romance
Patchouli	X	Love, passion
Periwinkle		Love, purification,i
Pine	X	Purification, Horned God, protection
Plantain		Increases the power of magick
Red Clover		Love, protection
Rose	X	Goddess, love, consecration
Rosemary	X	Cleansing, purification, protection
Sage	X	Cleansing, purification
Sandalwood X	X	High spiritually
Savory		Passion
Tarragon		Sexual
Thyme		Love, protection
Turmeric		Safe journey, protection
Valerian		Purification, protection

Incense Recipes

Altar
3 parts sandalwood
1 part frankincense
1 part myrrh
1/2 part lavender flowers
1/2 part hyssop herb
1/2 part rosemary
Rose oil
Lily oil
Orris root oil
Add the oils to your liking.

Earth
3 parts cedar
1 part oak tree wood
2 parts amber resin
1 part vetivert
1part corn silk
Patchouly oil
Sweet pea oil
Jasmine oil

Air
3 parts pine wood
1 parts Lemon Grass
1 part marjoram
1 part lavendar
1 part benzoin
Lilly of the valley oil
Lemon verbena oil

Fire
3 parts Walnut wood or ground walnut nut shells
1 part cedar
1 part damiana
1/2 part clove
1/2 part coriander
1 part bay
1 1/2 parts dragon's blood resin
Carnation oil
Orange oil

Water
3 parts sandalwood
1 part comfrey
1/2 part orris root
2 parts rose petals
2 part myrrh

Spirit
2 parts chamomile
3 parts sandalwood
1 part violet flowers
1 part rosemary
1/2 part frankincense

$^{1}/_{2}$ part ground cardamom seed
Gardenia oil
Lilac oil
Vanilla oil

$^{1}/_{2}$ myrrh
Gardenia oil

Goddess
3 parts sandalwood
1 part crushed cardamom seed
2 part chamomile
2 parts red rose petals
1 part dragons blood resin
1 part frankincense
Sweet pea oil
Lotus oil
Vanilla oil

Horned God
3 parts cedar wood
2 parts pine needles
2 parts bay leaves
1 part oak moss
1 part benzoin gum
1 part dragons blood
Patchouli oil
Frankincense oil
Clove oil

Sabbat Incense

Yule
3 parts pine needles
1 part ground Juniper berries
1 part allspice ground
1 part rosemary
1 part pine resin
1 part frankincense
Orrisroot oil
Sandalwood oil

Imbloc/Candlemas
2 parts pine wood sawdust
$1^{1}/_{2}$ parts birch wood dust
1 part wormwood power
1 part tansy
1 part heather
2 parts benzoin
Lily of the valley oil
Lotus oil

Spring Equinox
Equal parts ash and birch wood
1 part apple bark
1 part tansy
2 parts frankincense
Lemon verbena oil
Sweet pea oil
Lilac oil

Beltane
3 parts oak wood dust
2 part rose petals
1 part oak moss ground
2 parts dragon's blood
1 part frankincense
Violet oil
Rose oil

Summer Solstice
3 parts red sandalwood
2 parts frankincense
1 part chamomile
1/2 part angelica Root
Sweet orange oil
Sweet Pea oil

Lammas
2 parts sandalwood
1 part cedar wood
1 part corn silk
1 part benzoin
1 part frankincense
Orris root oil
Jasmine oil

Autumn Equinox
2 parts apple wood
1 part benzoin
1 part myrrh
1/2 part poppy seeds
1/2 ground clove
1 part bay laurel
Honeysuckle oil
Carnation oil

Samhain
2 parts sandalwood
1 part myrrh
1/2 part galangal root
1/2 part vervain
1 crushed dried apple
Rose geranium oil
Rosemary oil

Making your Personal Amulet

An amulet is something you wear all the time for protection, psychic awareness, good luck, etc. You can buy many different kinds of amulets from pentagrams to intricate designs. We are very different from each other, so it makes sense to formulate your own amulet, incorporating what is important to you.

Begin by researching symbols used for protection. Most popular is the pentagram, but if you take it a bit further you can find many attractive symbols, such as Celtic runes, God and Goddess symbols, and so on. It is an interesting journey searching for the symbols you relate to. Look into your own heritage and learn about the gods and goddesses you are closely attuned with. Write down all the different symbols you find and make note of their meaning. This will be important when choosing certain ones to incorporate into your amulet. There is a way of discovering your personal symbol in the universe. This is one you will want to use as a focal point in making your design. We start this process by working with numerology.

Example:

Your name + your craft name: Patricia Carol Martin/Windsinger. If you use the chart in the "Choosing Your Magickal Name" section of this book, this name carries a total of 1. But each number is important in finding your personal symbol.

Patricia =5

Carol=4

Martin=4

Windsinger =6.

Thus, some of the numbers we can work with are 5, 4, 4 and 6.

Once you have your numbers, make note of them in your Book of Shadows. They will become useful in other projects. Say that Patricia is a Scorpio with a Libra rising and a Leo moon. If you have this information, great, but if you don't, then her astrological sign alone is useful. It is a good idea to have your astrological chart done. Knowing this information about yourself can be of great use. I highly recommend it.

For Patricia, we also have the three astrological symbols she can incorporate in her design if she chooses, as well as their numerological values. The numbers for these signs are: Scorpio falls in the tenth and eleventh month of the year, equaling 21 =3, Libra falls in the ninth and tenth month equaling 19=10=1, and Virgo falls in the eighth and ninth month, equaling 17=8. These numbers can be used as well. Make note of them in your Book of Shadows. Patricia's sun sign is Scorpio, which is ruled by the planet Mars. All the planets have a square of numbers that represent it. If we take the square of Mars, we can plot her numbers on it, which will form a symbol she can work with. Here are the planetary squares and the astrological signs they rule:

Planetary Squares

Square of Saturn

4	9	2
3	5	7
8	1	6

Square of Jupiter

4	14	15	1
9	7	6	12
5	11	10	8
16	2	3	13

Capricorn, Aquarius, Sagittarius, Pisces

Square of Mars

11	24	7	20	3
4	12	25	8	16
17	5	15	21	9
10	18	1	14	22
25	6	19	2	15

Square of the Sun

6	32	3	34	35	1
7	11	27	28	8	30
19	14	16	15	25	24
18	20	22	21	17	13
25	29	10	9	26	12
36	5	33	4	2	31

Scorpio, Aries Leo

Square of Venus

22	47	16	41	10	35	4
5	23	43	17	42	11	29
30	6	24	49	18	36	12
13	31	7	25	43	19	37
38	14	32	1	26	44	20
21	39	8	33	2	27	45
46	15	40	9	34	3	28

Taurus, Libra

Square of Mercury

8	58	59	5	4	62	63	1
49	15	14	52	53	11	10	56
41	23	22	44	45	19	18	48
32	34	35	29	28	38	39	25
40	26	27	37	36	30	31	33
17	47	46	20	21	43	42	24
9	55	54	12	13	51	50	16
64	2	3	61	60	6	7	57

Libra, Taurus Gemini, Virgo

Square of Luna

37	78	29	70	21	62	13	54	5
6	38	79	30	71	22	63	14	46
47	7	39	80	31	72	23	55	15
16	48	8	40	81	32	64	24	56
57	17	49	9	41	73	33	65	25
26	58	18	50	1	42	74	34	66
67	27	59	10	51	2	43	75	35
36	68	19	60	11	52	3	44	76
77	28	69	20	61	12	53	4	45

Cancer

If you would like more information about the planetary squares, I can refer you to the book, *The Golden Dawn*, by Israel Regardie, Chapter on Talismans, pages 479 through 504.

The numbers we can plot for Patricia on the Mars square are the numbers for her names, which are: 5, 4, 4 and 6. Then for her astrological data, 3, 9 and 8. Her birthday is October 29, 1974. The birth date works out to be 10, 29 and 1974. When it is added together it comes out to be 60; this equals 6. We always go to the lowest denominator. So for the second sigil on the same square are the numbers 3, 9, 8 and 6. This will carry the vibrations of her names, birthday and astrological data.

To review: Start by plotting your name numbers. Then start another sigil on the same square for the astrological and birthday numbers.

To show the beginning, start with a small circle and end with a dash. This shows you the beginning and end. This is her personal symbol.

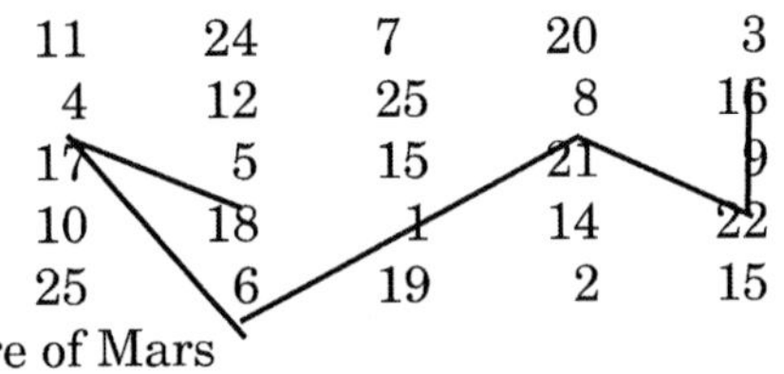

Square of Mars

This is the sigil for Patricia. She could place one over the other if she likes, creating a stronger vibration. This is what she would meditate on to receive her personal symbol.

Patricia is very much in tune with the crescent moon, so this would be one of her symbols. Let's look at what we have to work with.

To start, draw a circle, a square or a pyramid, or whatever symbol you are in tune with as a base. Place in the center the two sigils from the planetary square, either side by side or one over the other.

Now she would take this and place it to her third eye, which is between her eyebrows. She then needs to close her eyes and asks the question, "What is my personal symbol in this universe?" Then she must wait for a symbol to form in her mind. This is her personal power symbol in the universe. This symbol should be put on the other side of the design along with other symbols that are important to her, which could even be a family symbol. For Patricia, we place a pentagram and a crescent moon.

When she has the pendant made it should look something like this:

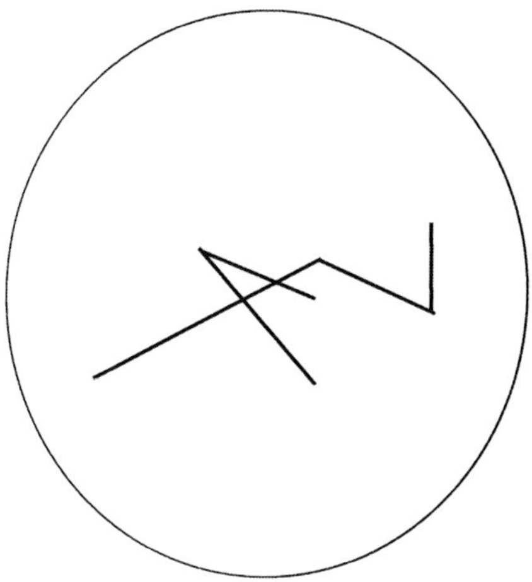

It is now time for you to make your own. This will be a very special pendant you will use for protection and the gaining of universal knowledge. Remember to consecrate it before you put it on. As you wear it you will charge it with your life force.

Animals, Our Familiars

Sometimes we come across an animal or bird that touches our hearts in a special way. It is almost like meeting a family member from another time. The bond is great and difficult to put into words, but you can surely feel it. This animal is your familiar. You can have more then one in your life, but usually only one at a time. They are with you to help you with your magick and life. In ancient folklore is said that animal familiars contain the spirits of the fae or the faery world. In others it is the mighty dead of the craft. What and who they are we can never be sure, but the bond we have with them is strong. Such is the story of me and Molly Malone.

Molly is a 104-pound Rottweiler who is happier than any being can be when I come home. I call her my love dog. We had a special bond from the first minute I saw her. She was the runt of the litter, much smaller then her eight brothers and sisters. There was something magical about her. My daughter-in-law Michelle was a breeder of Rots at the time. She told me she had a puppy for me. Since I had two other dogs I didn't think another large dog would be a good idea. But something made me travel more than an hour to South Miami to see this puppy. She was a little loner like myself. She was a Taurus birth sign, which is a very good combination for me as far as getting along. One of the unique things about Rottweilers is their puppy's look like baby bears. Molly could fit in the palm of my hands. I sat in wonderment of her, stroking her as I held her and watched her fall asleep on her back in my hands. I knew this was my dog and that this wouldn't be the only life we would be together. There was an instant bond. Amazingly, all of her brothers and sisters came down with Parvo and died shortly after I took her home. That was very sad, but it told me I was meant to have her.

This bond has grown over the seven years we have been together. When I do healings, she sits by my feet and lends her energies. If I have a circle, she always wants to come into it. When I'm not feeling well she will not leave my side for a moment. She always knows when something is up. When I have to travel, at least two weeks before she knows I'm going away. It is always a difficult time when I travel. At night she sleeps by the front door until I come home. Recently she became ill and I had to take her to the animal hospital. I could feel her emotions. We communicated with each other telepathically.

It's an amazing relationship having a familiar, but it is a responsibility. To lose a familiar is extremely painful, but they always come back to you either in this life or the next. There is a ritual you can do with your animal when you know it is your familiar.

Animal Bonding Ritual

It is best to erect your temple in an area your pet is familiar with. This ritual should only be between yourself and your animal. If you have a small pentagram you can attach to the collar. Place it on your altar. Have their favorite treat as their part of the cakes and wine ceremony. Have a statue of Goddess Diana if you have a dog, or a goddess associated with dogs. If you have a cat, then the Egyptian Goddess Bast would be a good statue to have on your altar. Erect your temple in the usual manner. Add to the calling of the guardians: "*Witness all, the bonding of myself and my familiar* __________." Now return to the center of the altar. Take up the wand and retrace the circle while walking with your animal. Walk your familiar around the circle three times, saying:

"*Around the circle three shall be,*
Our spirits travel for eternity,
Along the way we came together,
To learn and share and love forever."
"*So mote it be.*"

Return to the center of the altar and say your familiar's name three times. Give them a treat.

Sit and hold the animal on your lap. Close your eyes and visualize what their spirit truly looks like. Attach a silver thread from your solar plexus to theirs.

If you have a small pentagram, place it on their collar. If the animal doesn't wear a collar, visualize a pentagram on their chest and see it becoming part of their being.

Make an offering to the Goddess in both your names and ask for her guidance.

Then say to your familiar:

"*Always will I be there for you, we are bonded together in spirit.*
Always shall we connect with each other from lifetime to lifetime in need and in joy. So mote it be."

It is time to close the circle and bid the guardians farewell

Chapter 9

Meditations

Visiting the Gods and Goddess

In this chapter you will find different meditations in creating a relationship with the goddess and gods. Everyone has a different image of her or him. And you need to tune into your personal image so you can connect with them more easily.

There are many goddesses and many pythons for you to work with. All are the same goddess but different aspects of her. It is a good thing to get to know as many as you can.

In our lives there are lessons we need to learn and grow with. Sometimes it helps to tune into a particular aspect of the Goddess that can help us understand the lesson. Then the lessons are much easier to endure. For instance, if I have a lesson of survival ahead of me, I will visit with White Buffalo Calf Woman. She came for the survival of the Sioux nation. If I need to face a challenge and transformation in my life, then I would work with Goddess Inanna. She is well known in the Mesopotamian area of the ancient world.

The meditations you will experience now will be with different aspect of the goddesses and gods. This is so you feel the different energies of each. Working with the gods and goddess through meditation gives you the ability to tune into the answers from within.

It is best to make your own tapes of these meditations, playing soft meditative music in the background.

Pick a time of day when you know you won't be disturbed. Unplug the telephone, dim the lights, burn some incense and light a candle. You always want to create an atmosphere that is conducive to opening up your spiritual self.

Sit in a comfortable position with your limbs relaxed. Don't lie down if you have a tendency to fall asleep. Your induction should always be the same before you journey into a meditation. If you establish this, in time you will easily be able to put yourself into this state of mind.

Induction

Close your eyes and breathe deeply. Fill your lungs completely, holding your breath to the count of two heartbeats. Exhale completely, holding it out for two heartbeats. Continue this rhythmic breathing for at least ten full breaths. Now develop a comfortable breathing pattern. Feel your body relaxing. If you had a stressful day, go further with relaxing your body. Imagine your feet resting on a soft pink cloud. Whatever the pink touches it relaxes that part completely. Nothing can resist it. It naturally releases all tension. As you breathe in, the pink enters the bottom of your feet relaxing your toes and arches, and moves up relaxing your ankles. Feel it moving up into your calves, over your knees and up into your thighs. You can feel your legs letting go. Now feel it moving into your buttocks, your stomach and into your chest, relaxing everything as it gently moves through your body. Feel it moving up your spine into your neck, around your shoulders and into your face, removing all stress as it enters your scalp. Everything is now completely relaxed and you are ready to begin. It is time to turn on your tape and take your journey.

Earth Moon Meditation

Close your eyes and listen closely to the words of our great mother and follow.

"From the beginning my heartbeat and rhythm have formed the rhythms of all life as you know it. From the beginning of time until time has fulfilled its destiny, I, Mother Earth and the Moon Goddess have lived in harmony as life has been created. All life is one and depends upon each other. Know this to be true and learn how to feel the oneness.

Lie upon my soft body and feel the life within me. Now tune into your own heartbeat and feel your own rhythm. Take a deep breath - deeper - and fill your lungs with the air that sustains your life. This is the same air that my trees provide for your survival. As you breath deeply you can feel yourself getting heavier. You feel the gravity pulling upon your body. Feel yourself sinking into me, into my body. Feel the coolness of my earth. There is no problem breathing here because we are all one. Now feel the other life forces in the earth. Feel your heartbeat and mine beating as one. All is in harmony and is balanced between us. Remember this feeling. And if a time comes when you need help to re-establish it, come and join me again, for I am always here.

Take a deep breath and feel yourself coming to the surface of my body. Be aware of the light of the moon shining on you. Breathe deeply and breathe in her light. Feel the energies of the moon permeating every cell of your body. You can feel the fluid in your body moving, ebbing and flowing like my oceans. This is the effect the moon has upon us.

I, as Mother Earth, cannot exist without her energies and force, as you feel now in your own body. It is the same with my fluids: the oceans, rivers and lakes. The forces of the moon have always affected the fluids of our bodies. I, the Earth Goddess, and the Moon Goddess and yourself are all one energy. All having its own purpose, but existing in each other's rhythm. Feel it, feel it all coming together. For we are all part of the universe, and each completes the whole.

Take a deep breath and feel yourself coming back to the now, back to this time, this place and this moment. When you are ready you can open your eyes.

A Visit with the Goddess

In this meditation you will open up to the Goddess and her energies. Relax yourself as directed in the previous passage and then take the journey.

Imagine yourself in a field of wildflowers. The scent is intoxicating. It is the dark of night and above you is the full moon shining in all her glory. You can feel her rays shinning upon your face and body. It gives you the sense of lightness. As you breathe in the scented air you feel yourself slowly lifting up into the night air. Floating up on the rays of the moon, soaring above the clouds to a special place on the other side of the moon. You can feel the breeze of the night flowing through your hair. Your spirit feels uplifted.

As you arrive on the other side of the moon you can see beneath you a forest. Feel yourself floating down gently as if you were a feather. As you land you can see many others who have come to visit with her. No, you are not alone and you are not the only one.

You follow the others through the forest and come to the foot of a hill that has a winding road leading to the top. You can't see what is above, but you can feel an incredible energy coming from there. Your heart is getting excited at the possibilities that await you. You are stopped by one of the guardians as you begin your journey up the hill. They are holding in their hands a large bowl of water. It is the first dew of spring. They motion you to sprinkle your face with the dew. You put your hands into the bowl to refresh yourself. It makes you feel so youthful and alive. Legend has it that to sprinkle your face with the first dew of spring ensures youth and beauty. The guardian steps aside for you to pass. As you look around you can see a slight glow coming from everything around you. It is only visible from the corner of your eye. You continue up the hill. Another guardian approaches holding a beautiful white flowing robe. You take it and put it on without hesitation. It is as soft as a cloud. There are sandals placed before you to step into. To your amazement, they fit as if they were made for you. You wonder how they could have known.

As you reach the top of the hill you can hear your name being spoken in a whisper. You can feel your heart beating with excitement. There, just ahead, is a ball of glowing light. As you approach the light it takes the form of a beautiful woman. Her arms are outstretched to welcome you. She embraces you as you draw near. You feel the most overwhelming feeling of love that it brings tears to your eyes. This is the purest form of love you have ever felt. She calls you by another name. Remember this name if you can. She sits upon a magnificent throne of flowers. You sit beside her and lay your head upon her knees. She strokes your hair like a loving mother would. You can feel yourself falling into a restful sleep.

As you awaken you find yourself back where you began this journey. Can you remember the name you were called? You can revisit the Goddess for her council in the future if you need. She is always there for you. She was there at the beginning when you took your first breath, she will be there when your earthly journey is complete.

Hall of the Gods and Goddesses

In this meditation you will discover the goddess or the gods you are most in tune with. Once you have this information you will need to journey with them. Follow the introduction until you feel totally relaxed.

Visualize yourself in a great hall with walls of marble and ceilings that are three floors high. Before you are great, dark wooden double doors that reach as high as the ceiling. In the center of them is a massive golden door knocker. There are great paintings on the walls of the gods and goddesses from every known pantheon, as well as some never seen by humans from other planets and dimensions. You have a feeling of awe as you look around. Behind the door is another world. It is a little frightening for you to approach the doors, but it all awaits you.

You realize that you are connected to all the gods and goddesses, so the fear begins to leave. There in front of the doors is a pair of shoes. They are the most beautiful shoes you have ever seen. They were made for your feet on the astral at the time of your birth. They have grown as you grew, so they fit your feet perfectly. These shoes are a key for you to enter the hall of the goddesses and gods. This is where it all began. It has always been here waiting for you.

Put the shoes on. As you walk close to the doors they open for you. As you step through the doorway you find yourself in another time and place. It is an incredible sight. There are statues of the goddesses and gods everywhere you look. There are trees and flowers around them. It is an enchanting place. The colors and some of the flowers are like none you have ever seen. As you walk you can feel a pull to some of the statues. Stop and read the plaques beneath these statues. This will tell you about them.

There is a place for your hand. If you place it in the form you will be able to feel their essence flow through your body. As you do this, the most miraculous sensation flows into you and circulates throughout your body. Its like nothing you have ever felt.

There are others that call to you. Walk over to them and place your hand in their form. What an incredible feeling. Remember those who called to you. Remember the sensations you felt. These are the higher beings you will journey with. They have something they wish to teach you.

It's time to return. You may come back when you feel you need to connect. As you walk through the doors they close behind you. As you walk away from the doors the shoes disappear and return to their place by the doors for your return. Its time to return to the present. Breathe deeply and bring yourself back to this time, this place and this moment.

Visit with White Buffalo Calf Woman

Breathe deeply and follow the relaxing introduction as above until you are ready begin your journey.

It is early morning and you are walking through a park. Suddenly a misty fog begins to roll in, slowly covering everything. You can't see anything around you but the dense fog. It is almost as though you walked into a cloud. You begin to feel a change of energy. As you listen you can hear the call of the wind. You begin to hear what sounds like voices. Follow the sound. Slowly the mist begins to disappear and you find yourself in a forest that is very different from the park you were walking in. You don't feel afraid, as you are so overcome by the wonderment of the beauty that surrounds you. The air is clear and clean, somehow different from what you are used to. You can hear a sound of drums in the distance. You know now you must have stepped back in time or into another world.

This is a time when Indians were free to roam as they pleased. As you look down at yourself you realize you have changed as well. Your skin is a rich reddish brown, and the clothes you are wearing are made from animal skins. Your hair is long and dark. You touch it and feel feathers there. You begin to feel a pull, so you follow where it takes you. You feel a sense of spirit all around. It is strong. You are walking in the direction of the force pulling you. Once again you come to an area shrouded in mist, but this time it carries someone or something toward you. Some of the mist clears, and directly in your path is a beautiful snow-white buffalo calf. The whiteness of the calf glows, and as the calf looks up at you she begins to change before your eyes.

Suddenly, before you is a beautiful Indian maiden with long black hair. She has deep-set black eyes and high, prominent cheekbones. In her hand is a pipe made of red clay with feathers and colored beads hanging from it. She holds it out to you and calls you by another name. You look at her, not sure whether it is you she is calling. She calls out the name again and then a third time, until there is no doubt she is calling you by your name in that lifetime. She instructs you in the naming ceremony and tells you this is your name to use whenever you want to contact her. She speaks to you about the earth and how you are one with it. She speaks of how all things are part of the earth. She tells you how people hurt themselves when they hurt the earth and asks you to pass this knowledge on to those you know. She then hands you the sacred pipe.

You smoke the pipe with her, and it is like inhaling sweet air. It is a very pleasant sensation. In the smoke you can see a vision. Remember the vision.

Slowly she begins to change back into the beautiful white buffalo calf, and the mist begins to roll in and takes her away. You are not sure if the vision is real or just a thought, but you can still feel her energy. Take three deep breaths and feel yourself coming back to the present. Bring yourself back to this time, this place and this moment. When you are ready, open your eyes.

Visit with Goddess Bridget

Follow the induction as above, and when you feel yourself totally relax begin the journey.

Visualize yourself in a field of wildflowers in a time long ago. To your left is a low mountainous area topped with beautiful purple heather. Its scent fills the air with its sweetness, and you are in awe of its beauty. To your right is a forest of oaks and ash trees filled with leaves of every shade of green. The bark of the trees is a dark brown, and the contrast is breathtaking. The trees are massive. Everything is fresh with the evening dew. You can see a well-worn winding road leading deep into the forest. It looks as if it has been there since the beginning of time.

Follow this trail into the forest. As you do your clothes change to a white flowing robe, and there is a wreath of flowers or leaves in your hair. You feel excitement building because you can sense that something very special awaits up ahead. You feel no fear, just pure delight. You begin to see others dressed as you are carrying lighted white candles. You are able to hear them chanting in low voices as you follow them deep into the forest. Up ahead you can see an opening to a cave that goes down into the ground. As you pass through the entrance someone hands you a lighted candle. Up ahead you can see three wells. They are sacred to the triple-goddess Bridget. It has been said they possess healing powers.

For thousands of years people have come to this place to honor the great mother who empowers them with healing energies and the ability to foresee the future through intuition. As the chanting builds a beautiful glow forms over the sacred well in the center. It begins to take form until it reveals the beautiful goddess Bridget. You can feel the overpowering energies that emanate from her. As the people go to the well and drink the water, Bridget touches each one on the forehead. When it is your turn to drink the water, you notice it is so pure it's almost sweet. You feel a little lightheaded at first, but the feeling quickly fades. Now you understand why they say water is the wine of the gods.

The goddess touches you on the forehead, and you can feel a surge of energy going through your body. Two other forces begin to form over the other sacred wells. One is a beautiful young maiden and the other is a very old woman. The maiden goddess is filled with hope, and the wise ancient mother is filled with the knowledge of the universe. They have the powers of beauty, healing and understanding. They place their hands in the wells and swirl the water three times sun-wise to bless the wells. Slowly they begin to become transparent and fade. Each person places their lighted candle at the well's edge and a wreath of flowers is placed on them. One by one they put their hands in the other two wells, swirling them three times in honor of the triple goddess.

They put some of the water on their faces and begin to chant: "Beauty is mine, healing throughout time, prophecy for all humans divine." Finally, you are beckoned to do the same. You join them in the chanting, feeling the energy flowing through you. You have the ability to heal yourself and others. You have the beauty of the Goddess shining through your eyes and the ability to see things to come. Work with your gifts, for this is the part of you that is the Goddess. It is time to return. Slowly all proceed out of the cave and through the forest until you return to the field of wildflowers. Close your eyes and take three deep breaths, and bring yourself back to the present, back to this place and this time. And when you are ready you can open your eyes.

The Best Wiccan Suppliers I know

Enchanted Forest Books and Gifts
11326 Seminole Blvd
Largo
Florida, 33778
USA
www..enchantedshop.com

This is an online store that is run by a priestesses of the craft. They have just about everything you can imagine from everything renaissance to books, tools, robes, herbs, oils, jewelry, etc.

Capall Bann Publishing
Auton Farm, Milverton
Somerset, TA4 1NE
England
www.capallbann.co.uk

This is one of the best sources of information on the craft.

Azure Green/Abyss Distribution
P. O. Box 48
Middlefield
Ma 01243-0048
USA
413-623-2155
www.AzureGreen.com

One of the very best suppliers of Craft Books, Tools, Jewelry and Music.

In Conclusion

There is so much to learn. That is one of the greatest things about the craft, seeing the world through different eyes. It is like waking up from a long dream. In thirty odd years I feel like I've experienced and learned many things that help make my life. I know I am more tolerant and accepting of people from other paths. I learned the value of life on every level, be it human, animal or vegetable. Yet I still feel as though I am at the beginning. There is so much more to learn. I know I'll be back to the earth for the rest of my lessons. There is just too much to understand in one lifetime. In that knowledge, I am comforted. Wicca is an amazing way of life, and I thank the Goddess. She turned the light on my path. So mote it be.

To be continued ....

A Selection of Witchcraft Books Published by Capall Bann:

Lid Off The Cauldron - A Handbook For Witches by Patricia Crowther

We are delighted to make this classic book available again. Patricia Crowther, a practising witch since 1960, lifts the lid off the cauldron of witchcraft and reveals some fascinating ingredients. She explores the history of the Craft and the methods and theory behind magic and initiation. Patricia details spells, chants, prayers, methods of divination and ancient symbols, combined with the wisdom and experience of a leading, knowledgeable witch who has had a high standing in witchcraft since the time of the revival in the early '60s. ISBN 186163 032 8 £10.95

From Stagecraft to Witchcraft - The Early Years of A High Priestess by Patricia Crowther

Patricia Crowther is known world-wide as a leading light in present-day witchcraft, having lead the Sheffield Coven for 40 years which has advanced many members to form their own covens, forming an incredible network. In this fascinating and enlightening book, Patricia tells of her early years, her successful stage career throughout the UK, her marriage to Arnold Crowther with whom she worked in entertainment and magic and, her friendship with Gerald Gardner, the leading figure in the renaissance of witchcraft, and thereby Paganism in the present day. Illustrated with many previously unseen photographs. ISBN 186163 1634 £10.95

The Zodiac Experience - Initiation Through the Twelve Signs - The Girdle of Venus by Patricia Crowther

"In the Zodiac Experience, Patricia Crowther presents a unique method of self initiation directly linked with the Sun's position in the zodiac. An imaginative, refreshing concept." Scott Cunningham. ***"Patricia Crowther's book provides a wonderful attunement with the earth - through the heavens - by way of magical procedure. The Zodiac Experience is exactly that - a living experience. It is an ongoing initiatory process that can be lived over several years, giving an overview of each astrological sign, bringing them to life with stories from many myths and legends and offering rituals that contain powerful visualisations. Here is a zodiac that can be truly appreciated."*** Ray Buckland ISBN 186163 1286 £11.95

A Witch's Kitchen Val Thomas

A Witch's Kitchen is about real, practical witchcraft. Covering such topics as food, drinks, herb lore, lotions and potions, shapeshifting, incenses, spinning, weaving, using natural dyes, making candles and working with fire, understanding plant spirits and consulting plant oracles, it forms a lively blend of everyday and magical information, which is up-to-date, yet well grounded in myth and tradition. It includes personal, often humourous, accounts of real incidents, which give a good feel for what life as a modern witch is actually like. The book has a strong awareness of the environmental and moral issues facing modern witches and an optimistic outlook, which will encourage and inspire the experienced witch as well as those who are new to the Craft.
ISBN 186163 1596 £13.95

FREE DETAILED CATALOGUE

Capall Bann is owned and run by people actively involved in many of the areas in which we publish. A detailed illustrated catalogue is available on request, SAE or International Postal Coupon appreciated. **Titles can be ordered direct from Capall Bann, post free in the UK** (cheque or PO with order) or from good bookshops and specialist outlets.

A Breath Behind Time, Terri Hector
A Soul is Born by Eleyna Williamson
Angels and Goddesses - Celtic Christianity & Paganism, M. Howard
The Art of Conversation With the Genius Loci, Barry Patterson
Arthur - The Legend Unveiled, C Johnson & E Lung
Astrology The Inner Eye - A Guide in Everyday Language, E Smith
Auguries and Omens - The Magical Lore of Birds, Yvonne Aburrow
Asyniur - Women's Mysteries in the Northern Tradition, S McGrath
Beginnings - Geomancy, Builder's Rites & Electional Astrology in the European Tradition, Nigel Pennick
Between Earth and Sky, Julia Day
Book of the Veil , Peter Paddon
The Book of Seidr, Runic John
Caer Sidhe - Celtic Astrology and Astronomy, Michael Bayley
Call of the Horned Piper, Nigel Jackson
Can't Sleep, Won't Sleep, Linda Louisa Dell
Carnival of the Animals, Gregor Lamb
Cat's Company, Ann Walker
Celtic Faery Shamanism, Catrin James
Celtic Faery Shamanism - The Wisdom of the Otherworld, Catrin James
Celtic Lore & Druidic Ritual, Rhiannon Ryall
Celtic Sacrifice - Pre Christian Ritual & Religion, Marion Pearce
Celtic Saints and the Glastonbury Zodiac, Mary Caine
Circle and the Square, Jack Gale
Come Back To Life, Jenny Smedley
Compleat Vampyre - The Vampyre Shaman, Nigel Jackson
Creating Form From the Mist - The Wisdom of Women in Celtic Myth and Culture, Lynne Sinclair-Wood
Crystal Clear - A Guide to Quartz Crystal, Jennifer Dent
Crystal Doorways, Simon & Sue Lilly
Crossing the Borderlines - Guising, Masking & Ritual Animal Disguise in the European Tradition, Nigel Pennick
Dragons of the West, Nigel Pennick

Earth Dance - A Year of Pagan Rituals, Jan Brodie
Earth Harmony - Places of Power, Holiness & Healing, Nigel Pennick
Earth Magic, Margaret McArthur
Egyptian Animals - Guardians & Gateways of the Gods, Akkadia Ford
Eildon Tree (The) Romany Language & Lore, Michael Hoadley
Enchanted Forest - The Magical Lore of Trees, Yvonne Aburrow
Eternal Priestess, Sage Weston
Eternally Yours Faithfully, Roy Radford & Evelyn Gregory
Everything You Always Wanted To Know About Your Body, But So Far Nobody's Been Able To Tell You, Chris Thomas & D Baker
Experiencing the Green Man, Rob Hardy & Teresa Moorey
Face of the Deep - Healing Body & Soul, Penny Allen
Fairies and Nature Spirits, Teresa Moorey
Fairies in the Irish Tradition, Molly Gowen
Familiars - Animal Powers of Britain, Anna Franklin
Flower Wisdom, Katherine Kear
Fool's First Steps, (The) Chris Thomas
Forest Paths - Tree Divination, Brian Harrison, Ill. S. Rouse
From Past to Future Life, Dr Roger Webber
From Stagecraft To Witchcraft, , Patricia Crowther
Gardening For Wildlife Ron Wilson
God Year, The, Nigel Pennick & Helen Field
Goddess on the Cross, Dr George Young
Goddess Year, The, Nigel Pennick & Helen Field
Goddesses, Guardians & Groves, Jack Gale
Handbook For Pagan Healers, Liz Joan
Handbook of Fairies, Ronan Coghlan
Healing Book, The, Chris Thomas and Diane Baker
Healing Homes, Jennifer Dent
Healing Journeys, Paul Williamson
Healing Stones, Sue Philips
Herb Craft - Shamanic & Ritual Use of Herbs, Lavender & Franklin
Hidden Heritage - Exploring Ancient Essex, Terry Johnson
Hub of the Wheel, Skytoucher
In and Out the Windows, Dilys Gator
In Search of Herne the Hunter, Eric Fitch
In Search of the Green Man, Peter Hill
Inner Celtia, Alan Richardson & David Annwn
Inner Mysteries of the Goths, Nigel Pennick
Inner Space Workbook - Develop Through Tarot, Cat Summers & Julian Vayne
In Search of Pagan Gods, Teresa Moorey
Intuitive Journey, Ann Walker Isis - African Queen, Akkadia Ford
Journey Home, The, Chris Thomas
Kecks, Keddles & Kesh - Celtic Lang & The Cog Almanac, Bayley
Language of the Psycards, Berenice
Legend of Robin Hood, The, Richard Rutherford-Moore

Lid Off the Cauldron, Patricia Crowther
Light From the Shadows - Modern Traditional Witchcraft, Gwyn
Living Tarot, Ann Walker
Lore of the Sacred Horse, Marion Davies
Lost Lands & Sunken Cities (2nd ed.), Nigel Pennick
The Magic and Mystery of Trees, Teresa Moorey
Magic For the Next 1,000 Years, Jack Gale
Magic of Herbs - A Complete Home Herbal, Rhiannon Ryall
Magical Guardians - Exploring the Spirit and Nature of Trees, Philip Heselton
Magical History of the Horse, Janet Farrar & Virginia Russell
Magical Lore of Animals, Yvonne Aburrow
Magical Lore of Cats, Marion Davies
Magical Lore of Herbs, Marion Davies
Magick Without Peers, Ariadne Rainbird & David Rankine
Masks of Misrule - Horned God & His Cult in Europe, Nigel Jackson
Medicine For The Coming Age, Lisa Sand MD
Medium Rare - Reminiscences of a Clairvoyant, Muriel Renard
Menopausal Woman on the Run, Jaki da Costa
Mind Massage - 60 Creative Visualisations, Marlene Maundrill
Mirrors of Magic - Evoking the Spirit of the Dewponds, P Heselton
The Moon and You, Teresa Moorey
Moon Mysteries, Jan Brodie
Mysteries of the Runes, Michael Howard
Mystic Life of Animals, Ann Walker
New Celtic Oracle The, Nigel Pennick & Nigel Jackson
Oracle of Geomancy, Nigel Pennick
Pagan Feasts - Seasonal Food for the 8 Festivals, Franklin & Phillips
Paganism For Teens, Jess Wynne
Patchwork of Magic - Living in a Pagan World, Julia Day
Pathworking - A Practical Book of Guided Meditations, Pete Jennings
Personal Power, Anna Franklin
Pickingill Papers - The Origins of Gardnerian Wicca, Bill Liddell
Pillars of Tubal Cain, Nigel Jackson
Places of Pilgrimage and Healing, Adrian Cooper
Planet Earth - The Universe's Experiment, Chris Thomas
Practical Divining, Richard Foord
Practical Meditation, Steve Hounsome
Practical Spirituality, Steve Hounsome
Psychic Self Defence - Real Solutions, Jan Brodie
Real Fairies, David Tame
Reality - How It Works & Why It Mostly Doesn't, Rik Dent
Romany Tapestry, Michael Houghton
Runic Astrology, Nigel Pennick
Sacred Animals, Gordon MacLellan
Sacred Celtic Animals, Marion Davies, Ill. Simon Rouse
Sacred Dorset - On the Path of the Dragon, Peter Knight

Sacred Grove - The Mysteries of the Forest, Yvonne Aburrow
Sacred Geometry, Nigel Pennick
Sacred Nature, Ancient Wisdom & Modern Meanings, A Cooper
Sacred Ring - Pagan Origins of British Folk Festivals, M. Howard
Season of Sorcery - On Becoming a Wisewoman, Poppy Palin
Seasonal Magic - Diary of a Village Witch, Paddy Slade
Secret Places of the Goddess, Philip Heselton
Secret Signs & Sigils, Nigel Pennick
The Secrets of East Anglian Magic, Nigel Pennick
A Seeker's Guide To Past Lives, Paul Williamson
Seeking Pagan Gods, Teresa Moorey
A Seer's Guide To Crystal Divination, Gale Halloran
Self Enlightenment, Mayan O'Brien
Spirits of the Air, Jaq D Hawkins
Spirits of the Water, Jaq D Hawkins
Spirits of the Fire, Jaq D Hawkins
Spirits of the Aether, Jaq D Hawkins
Spirits of the Earth, Jaq D Hawkins
Stony Gaze, Investigating Celtic Heads John Billingsley
Stumbling Through the Undergrowth , Mark Kirwan-Heyhoe
Subterranean Kingdom, The, revised 2nd ed, Nigel Pennick
Symbols of Ancient Gods, Rhiannon Ryall
Talking to the Earth, Gordon MacLellan
Talking With Nature, Julie Hood
Taming the Wolf - Full Moon Meditations, Steve Hounsome
Teachings of the Wisewomen, Rhiannon Ryall
The Other Kingdoms Speak, Helena Hawley
Transformation of Housework, Ben Bushill
Tree: Essence of Healing, Simon & Sue Lilly
Tree: Essence, Spirit & Teacher, Simon & Sue Lilly
Tree Seer, Simon & Sue Lilly
Through the Veil, Peter Paddon
Torch and the Spear, Patrick Regan
Understanding Chaos Magic, Jaq D Hawkins
Understanding Past Lives, Dilys Gater
Understanding Second Sight, Dilys Gater
Understanding Spirit Guides, Dilys Gater
Understanding Star Children, Dilys Gater
The Urban Shaman, Dilys Gater
Vortex - The End of History, Mary Russell
Warp and Weft - In Search of the I-Ching, William de Fancourt
Warriors at the Edge of Time, Jan Fry
Water Witches, Tony Steele
Way of the Magus, Michael Howard
Weaving a Web of Magic, Rhiannon Ryall
West Country Wicca, Rhiannon Ryall